A Hundred Years on a Medieval Manor

Susannah Horne

The Cockerel Press

First published in 2022 by The Cockerel Press
Copyright © 2022 Susannah Horne

ISBN 978-1-909871-24-3

The Cockerel Press is an imprint of Dorking Museum and Heritage Centre,
The Old Foundry, 62 West Street, Dorking, RH4 1BS
www.dorkingmuseum.org.uk
admin@dorkingmuseum.org.uk

Printed and bound by Short Run Press Limited, Exeter

Acknowledgments and Illustrations

The author would like to thank the staff at the Surrey History Centre and the Arundel Castle archive, where most of the Dorking manorial records can be found.

The majority of the illustrations in this book are line drawings based on bas-de-page illuminations found in three medieval manuscripts: the Luttrell Psalter (Add MS 42130), the Queen Mary Psalter (Royal MS 6 E VII) and the Smithfield Decretals (Royal MS 10 E IV). All three works can be accessed via the British Library's digitised manuscripts website (bl.uk/manuscripts). The cover image is Add MS 42130/f.196v © British Library Board. The drawing on p.15 is based on the decorative capital on a Bristol charter (Bristol City Archive 01250); that on p.45 is based on an illustration in the 16thC Nuremberg House Book and that on p.71 is from an early 15thC missal (Pierpont Morgan MS M.146). The earl's seal (p.74) and the church's east window (p.118) were originally reproduced in Howard de Walden (1904) and SyAC XIV. The west window (also p.118) is taken from a watercolour by Edward Hassell (SHC 1867/17/1/9).

All the maps, bar one, are based on Beryl Higgins's rendering of the 1649 survey map, which can be accessed via Dorking Museum's website (dorkingmuseum.org.uk); the exception is the drawing on p.50, which is based on the Copperplate map of London.

Finally, the author would like to express her gratitude to Sue Horne for creating the original artworks found on pages 112, 117, 120 and 131 and for preparing the images of the church windows for reproduction.

Contents

A Note on Names

During the late 13th and 14th centuries, surnames became the norm in England. In Dorking, they were most commonly derived from the place someone came from; of the 244 second names mentioned in the 1282-3 court roll, 100 refer to places. These range from the very local (at Clerhole, at Holoweye, at Mesbroke or de la Garstone) to the slightly further afield (de Clandon, de Guldeford, de Kyngesfolde or de Newdigate). Occasionally, someone appears from outside the county, such as John de London (one of the millers) or, most exotic of all, Clerekyn de Florence (Henry de Sutbury's son-in-law). Thirty-nine of the names in the 1282-3 roll are based on someone's job, ranging from baker, butcher, carter or clerk to ironmonger, tailor or tanner. Surnames could also be derived from either Christian names or nicknames. Interestingly, some of the former were originally Anglo-Saxon, such as Godwyne, Harm, Osward or Siward. Others were Old Norse (Geffrey, Osbern or Thurbarn) or Anglo-Norman/Old French (Alard, Maynard or Moraunt). Nicknames tended to highlight the physical description of a person, particularly their hair colour or complexion.

This was a period of transition, when personal identifiers were settling down to become true surnames but the system was still in flux. This means that one can't assume that someone called 'at Stombelhole' was actually from there; it might have been his father or grandfather. Equally, someone called 'Fisher' was not necessarily a fishmonger nor a 'Tailor' working in the textile trade. Even personal nicknames could be deceptive. When Ralph le Buchiere appeared in a manorial document, he was also described as 'Ralph le Rede'. One might visualise a butcher with flaming red hair but, in fact, his brother was Thomas le Rede, who held 300 acres of land in villeinage from the earl. 'Le Rede' had obviously become a true surname, not a nickname.

An added confusion derives from the fact that medieval clerks wrote primarily in Latin and often spoke Anglo-Norman French. A nice example of the effect of this can be found in the 1263 Surrey Eyre, where the name of William Brekespere is rendered as 'Bruselaunce': a French translation in the middle of a Latin document. Surnames based on location tended to be expressed by clerks interchangeably using the English 'atte' or the French 'de la'. Thus, 'Alice atte Wode' and 'Alice de la Wode' refer to the same person. Alternatively, her surname might be written in Latin as 'de Bosco'; this wandering into Latin was particularly prevalent with names based on job titles, as when 'Smith' became 'Faber' or 'Skinner' became 'Peletor'. Different versions were often used in the same document, so the reader has to be constantly on guard. Sometimes, a true surname was used along with the person's actual job, as in records from the 1380s, when Laurence Ingylby was also referred to as Laurence Sherman. (A 'shearman' was a cloth worker.)

Christian names in this period, particularly for men, were not very varied. In contrast to the wide and inventive range of Anglo-Saxon names, the post-Conquest parent or godparent seems to have had a much narrower choice. This limited range is clearly demonstrated by the top ten names for men found in the Dorking court rolls: Gilbert, Henry, John, Peter, Richard, Robert, Roger, Thomas, Walter and William. Throughout the period covered by this book, John and William far outstrip the others, followed by Richard and Robert; by 1382, 28% of the men who appeared in the Dorking court roll were called 'John' and 14½% 'William'. There was a smattering of other male names in use on the manor (such as Adam, Geoffrey, Giles, Hugh, James, Laurence, Maurice, Ralph, Simon or Stephen) and, presumably, casual versions were also used, such as Jack for John, Harry for Henry or Wat for Walter. However, these tend not to show up in official documents.

Women's names appear much more rarely in the written record but Agnes and Alice were clearly the most popular female names in Dorking, followed by Isabelle and Margery. The complete list from all the sources used for this book is as follows: Agatha, Agnes, Alice, Amice, Avelina, Basilia, Beatrix, Bronild, Cecily, Christiana, Clarisse, Dionisia, Edith, Elizabeth, Emma, Felicia, Gunnild, Guthra, Hawise, Idonia, Isabelle, Joan, Juliana, Katherine, Letice, Lucy, Mabel, Margery, Marona, Matilda, Milsant, Petronilla, Rose and Sybil. Although much less frequently recorded than male names (many of the above only occur in the Poll Tax return of 1381), they do seem rather more varied than the men. 'Edith' is the only Anglo-

Saxon name to survive, while 'Gunnild' (originally a Norse name) was reliably popular on the manor, occurring throughout our period.

Women were usually identified by their relationship with a father or husband but some were given surnames, particularly if named in relation to their work. A list of alesellers will always include a number of women identified in this way and the 1381 Poll Tax return for Dorking includes eleven women listed in their own right, mostly as spinsters.

All in all, names in this period are a bit of a minefield, not least because medieval spelling was somewhat erratic and the same name may appear in many different guises. The most extreme example in the Dorking manorial records is the surname which has been rendered throughout this book simply as 'at Churchgate' but which appears in no less than nine possible combinations: atte/de/de la Churchegate, Chergate, Churgate, Cherchegate, Chertgate or even Cherhegate. The author has tried to be consistent with whichever version of a particular surname she has chosen and has used 'at' for 'atte' throughout. She refers frequently to 'surnames' but it should be borne in mind that true surnames were still in development during this period.

A Note on Dates

The manorial court year began at Michaelmas (29th September) and was dated according to the king's regnal year. Converting the latter to an annual year is not straightforward because the medieval year began in spring on Lady Day (25th March). Thus, the first court roll for Dorking spans 1282-3 but January, February and March took place in winter 1282, rather than 1283. Historians signify this by using the following convention: 1st January 1282/3.

Glossary

Advowson	the right to appoint a priest to the parish church
Affeerer	an appointee of the manor court in charge of financial matters
Attached	ordered to attend the manor court
Borough	see 'tithing'
Chevage	an annual payment for permission to live off-manor
Cotland	the smallest amount of land held by customary tenure
Cottar	the holder of a cotland
Cultor	part of a plough
Curtilage	plot of land on which a messuage is situated
Demesne	the lord's own land on the manor
Demised at farm	land or property leased for a fixed sum and term
Distrained	confiscation of goods ordered by the manor court
Essoin	excuse for not attending the manor court
Ferlingsman	the holder of a furlong
Forestalling	buying goods before the market opens, with a view to selling later at a higher price
Freehold	land tenure with very few services attached
Furlong	a quarter of a virgate
Glebe	land of the parish church intended to support the vicar
Headborough	leader of a tithing
Heriot	death duty, usually the deceased's best beast
Homage	all the attendees at the manor court
Love-day	a date for two parties to settle out of court
Merchet	the fee paid to allow an unfree person to marry whom they chose
Messuage	the dwelling house and outbuildings on a curtilage
Mill soke	the requirement to grind grain at the lord's mill
Murrain	an infectious animal disease
Perch	a measurment of land, either a quarter of a chain or 1/160th of an acre
Pinfold	an animal pound
Pledge	a guarantor at the manor court
Purpresture	permitted encroachment on the lord's land
Quitrent	money paid to release the purchaser from services associated with a property

Rod	a measurement of land, c.5½ yards
Stot	a small, cheap horse
Suit of court	the right and obligation to attend the manor court
Tallage	the lord's right to tax tenants at will
Tenement	a landholding
Tithing	a group of men bound together by mutual surety (known as a borough in Surrey)
View of Frankpledge	annual court where tithing matters were discussed and recorded
Villein	an unfree person
Virgate	a piece of land, usually 100 acres on Dorking manor
Virgater	the holder of a virgate
Waged his/her law	swearing on oath as to one's innocence, with three, six or twelve supporters doing the same
Waste	damaged or unproductive land
Weif	abandoned goods

Introduction

The medieval manor of Dorking was a large estate, covering more than 7,000 acres. Nine miles in length and three in breadth, it stretched from the greensand ridge of Ranmore in the north to the border of Sussex in the south. Two main roads ran through the manor, one from east to west, between Reigate and Guildford, and another south via Coldharbour and Ockley. The latter started in the town of Dorking, which guarded the geological feature now known as the 'Mole Gap'; strategically, this was the main approach to London from the south coast.

The aim of this book is to build a picture of the people who lived on the manor between the 1280s and the 1380s. At the top of the social hierarchy was the Earl of Surrey, who was lord of the manor. Dorking had been a royal estate until King William Rufus gave it to William de Warenne, the second earl. It was one of several de Warenne manors in Surrey, including Reigate, Shere and East Betchworth, which formed part of a vast landholding scattered throughout England, particularly in Norfolk and Sussex. It is doubtful whether any of the earls ever set foot in their manor of Dorking. The nearest of their residences was at Reigate castle.

The earl was represented by his steward, who was based at Reigate. He ran several nearby manors and was a man of substance in his own right. As well as the earl's own 'demesne' land, the manor was divided between freehold property and customary tenancies. There were also two pieces of land held by 'knight's fee', which originally meant that the service of an armed knight had to be made available to a superior lord but now involved payment of a pair of gilded spurs as rent. The freehold property was scattered throughout both town and manor; such land wasn't owned outright but was free of customary services or dues and could be inherited or granted elsewhere without the earl's permission. It was often held as an investment by people living outside the manor who rented their properties to others.

Thirty-eight plots of land were customary tenancies held by those who, as well as their rent, had to make a number of other payments to the earl and provide a wide range of agricultural work on his demesne land.

1

A map of Surrey, showing the hundred boundaries and key places mentioned in the text.

These varied in size, from a virgate or half a virgate to a furlong or half a furlong. A 'virgate' is a division of a 'hide' (an Anglo-Saxon landholding) and is usually taken to be about thirty acres. However, its size depended on the amount of land required to support a household. In Dorking, much of the land was (and still is) heavy clay: difficult to work, it dries out quickly in sunshine and is easily waterlogged in rain. This, together with extensive woodland, meant that a virgate may have been as much as 100 acres.[1] The poorest of the earl's tenants were the cottars, who held very small plots of land, mostly in or near the town. Both they and those who held the customary tenancies may also have been personally unfree. Historically referred to as 'villeins', these were people who couldn't leave the manor without permission and were subject to other legal restrictions.

------

[1] Based on a reference in the Extent to Chert being half a virgate or fifty acres.

Much of the available information about these people lies in documents drawn up to aid the running of the manor: sets of accounts, records of manorial courts and surveys of the estate. These documents provide details of how the earl's demesne land was farmed and the various ways he received income from his tenants. They are full of information about the residents of the manor; this is particularly true of the manor court, which had to be attended by all the customary tenants and those freeholders who had business there. However, these records were drawn up for a specific purpose by the earl's men and many residents do not appear in them. Other contemporary documents (such as taxation records) can supply additional information but some sections of society were routinely under-represented.

One very useful document was created in 1307. This was an 'extent' of the manor (referred to hereafter as 'the Extent'). It consisted of a description of the earl's demesne, a list of the customary tenants and cottars, giving us their names, their plots and all the payments and services they were expected to provide, and a list of the freeholders, their properties and the names of those from whom they had received them. All of which is very informative, giving a snapshot of life on the manor at a particular moment. However, caution must be applied as the document captures something which was already changing. Unfortunately, the original text doesn't survive, so the researcher has to work from a copy made in the late 16thC and notes made by William Bray, the famed antiquarian, in the early 19thC. His notes differ in some respects from the 16thC copy, so it seems likely he was working from the original. The 16thC clerk obviously had trouble reading some of the names and left out some details which were irrelevant to the running of a manor by his time. He also copied extracts from manor court rolls up to 1571, mostly to do with property transactions. Why he had been asked to undertake such a tedious task is unknown.

A survey of the manor was conducted in 1649 and was accompanied by a map (on which all the maps presented in this book are based). Many names had become attached to pieces of land by then, so this gives us a clear idea of how the manor was laid out and where the people named in the Extent lived. This information can be supplemented by details from property deeds and, of course, the manor court rolls.

For administrative purposes, the manor was divided into four tithings. In Surrey, tithings were known as 'boroughs'; in Dorking, they were called Chippingborough, Eastborough, Foreignborough and Waldeborough. 'Chipping' is derived from the Anglo-Saxon word for market (OE *ceopan*, 'to buy') and this borough was in the centre of town. Eastborough was, unsurprisingly, to the east, further along what is now called the High Street but used to be known as 'East Street'. 'Walde' simply means 'Weald' and covered the rural south of the manor. These were the original pre-Conquest boroughs, which were then joined by Foreignborough as a result of an increase in population during the first half of the 14thC. 'Foreign' meant 'outside the town' and comprised households in and around the Homwode (now Holmwood common), after which the tithing was later renamed. Each borough had an elected headborough, who presented misdemeanors at the annual View of Frankpledge. This was the court through which petty quarrels, trade regulations and repairs to the public roads were dealt with, usually via small fines. Other officials on the manor were the reeve, appointed yearly from among the customary tenants to run things day-to-day, and two beadles, elected from the same, to assist him.

The 'hundred years' to which this book's title refers lie between 1282 and 1381. These dates may seem strangely precise but they are driven by the documentary evidence. The earliest surviving manor court roll begins in September 1282 and ends the following September. Unfortunately, we do not have a complete run of court rolls for 14thC Dorking: the next two date from 1342 and 1344-5 and both are incomplete. A full year survives from 1365-6 and then, in the 1380s, the rolls become much more regular but much more repetitive. This has an impact on the way we can study the manor, as the kind of analysis made possible by a long run of consecutive records is not feasible. However, the snapshots provided by these surviving court rolls, supplemented by other contemporary documents, allow some valuable insights to be gathered.

The years between 1282 and 1381 span the reigns of Edwards I, II and III and Richard II. The beginning of this period, from the 1280s to the turn of the century, was noteable for good weather and abundant harvests. Unfortunately, this good fortune did not last: the first half of the 14thC has been described as 'perhaps the most difficult and hazardous episode in the annals of English agriculture'.[2] The weather deteriorated. Crop failures and disease among the livestock led to food shortages. There was famine throughout Europe, particularly between 1315 and 1322; this was followed by the Black Death, which hit England in 1348. Warfare was also a constant as English kings fought the Scots and the French, leading to increased taxation. Then, at the end of our period, came the 'Peasants' Revolt', that great upsurge of rebellion against a social order that sought to keep 'villeins' in their place.

However, as we will see, very little of this trouble is visible in Dorking's contemporary manorial documents. What they do provide is a series of glimpses into the lives of the people who lived and worked on the manor. Lifting the veil of clerkly Latin and the requirements of officialdom, the actions and occasionally the voices of Dorking residents in the late 13th and 14th centuries can be allowed to speak for themselves.

---

[2] Campbell (2000), p.23.

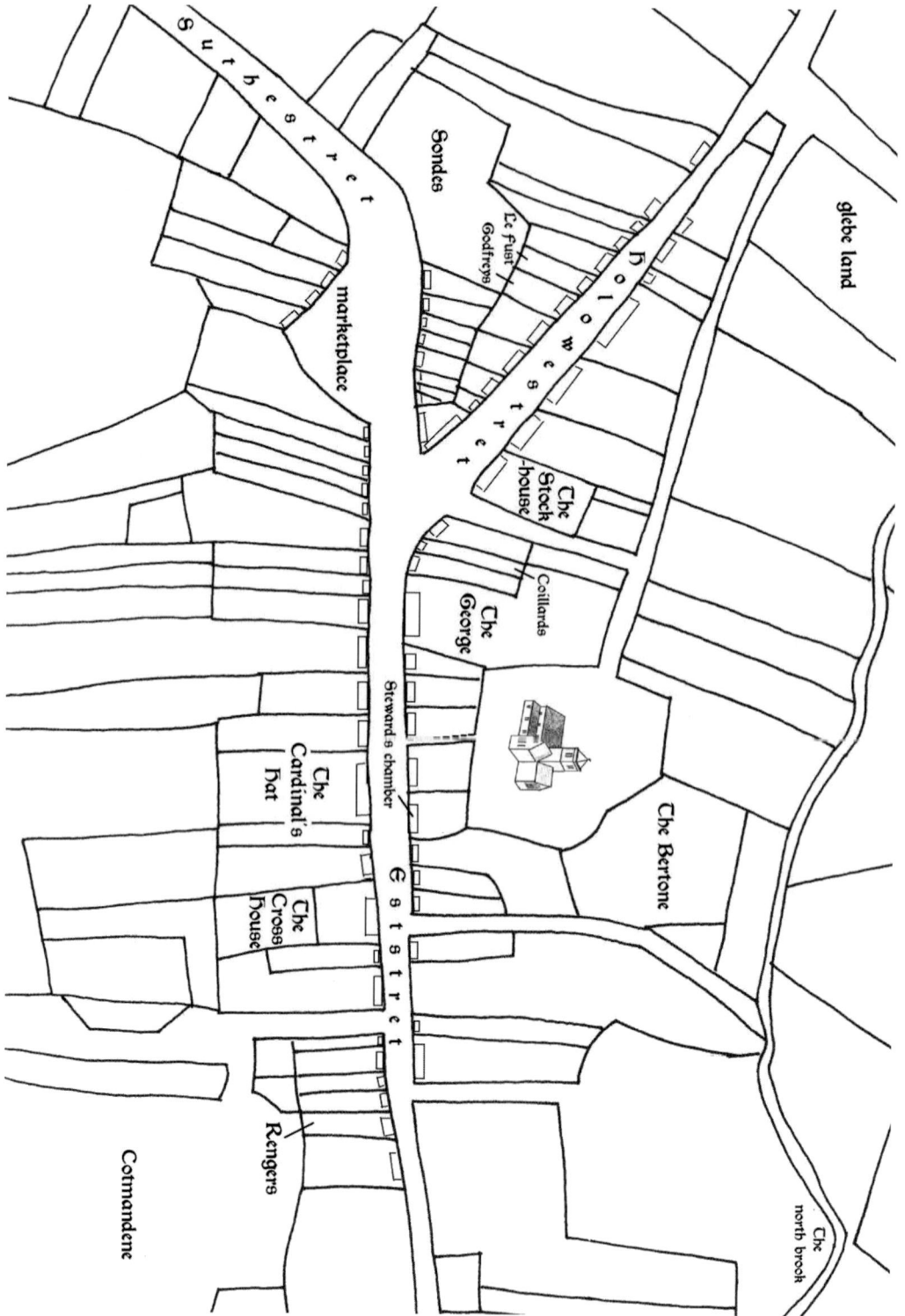

A plan of the centre of Dorking town. Only those properties whose location can be verified have been included.

Sutheestreet

Sondes

Le fust Godfreys

holowestreet

glebe land

marketplace

The Stock house

Coillards

The George

Steward's chamber

The Cardinal's hat

The Cross house

The Bertone

Eaststreet

Rengers

Cotmandene

The north brook

The First Twenty-five Years: 1282-1307

Every three weeks, Walter le Grant rode from Reigate to Dorking. In his capacity as steward to the Earl of Surrey and accompanied by his clerk and servants, he came to oversee the Dorking manor court. His journey took him along the King's Highway through Buckland and Betchworth and across the river Emele (now called the Mole). Then, at a fork in the road, he could either go right towards Leatherhead or on into Dorking.

The town which he approached was much smaller than its modern descendant but was laid out on the same pattern. As Walter rode down the high street, he would have passed small houses positioned on narrow plots of land, the buildings timber-framed, with wattle-and-daub walls and tiled roofs. On his left, Walter might have noticed the cottage occupied by Adam Renger and his son, William, just before a lane that branched off towards Cotmandene. However, Walter's business was on the other side of the street. The piece of land where the court was held was accessed via the way later called Mill Lane. At the end of the lane was the stream known then as the North Brook (now the Pippbrook) and on the opposite bank stood one of the earl's two watermills. The demesne land lay beyond, framed by the high ridge of Ranmore.

There was no manor house in Dorking but there was a building referred to as the 'steward's chamber'. This seems to have been on the high street, on one of five plots that lay in front of the churchyard. A narrow way between two of these properties gave access to the church (as it still does). Presumably, the steward and his entourage stabled their horses there before proceeding to the court.

The manor court was usually held on Monday, which was one of two weekly market days, the other being Thursday. The marketplace probably lay in South Street, near the point where it diverged from West Street (then called Suthestret and Holowestret).[3] The market would have been full of stalls and the town full of people buying and selling all kinds of goods and foodstuffs. This was the most populous part of Dorking, the market stalls being surrounded by buildings, many of them shops with a board at the

---

[3] At least, they were so called in the 1420s.

front that could be let down to form a counter. There was also a 'seld': a stone building containing a number of stalls. The business of the market was carried out at a property on the marketplace known as the 'Tolhous' and there was also a small lock-up called the 'Tun'.

As well as the three roads that met in the centre of town, there was another little lane that led north. If Walter had walked that way, he would quickly have emerged into the street which was prosaically known in later times as Back Lane and is now Church Street. Turning to the right, he would have seen the church, a large stone building with a tower. Turning left and strolling along the lane, he would have ended up back on Holowestret, with the glebe land and tithe barn to his right. From there, the King's Highway continued through Westcott and on to Guildford, via Wotton and Shere.

If, however, he had chosen to walk down South Street, the houses on either side would have quickly petered out as the road emerged into fields. Were he riding south, Walter then had a choice: he could either proceed down Claygate Lane towards the Innome and Homwode or he could take the King's Highway through Coldharbour and on towards Sussex. However, the steward usually had other business in Dorking. Walter and his clerk had a busy day ahead of them.

Riding into town.

At the Manor Court

The first court of the year was held on the 17th September 1282, which was a Thursday. This was unusual as proceedings usually took place on a Monday but no reason is given for the alteration. All customary tenants owed 'suit of court' as part of their tenancies and were expected to attend every session. So too were freeholders whose tenure included suit of court or who had business there, although it was possible to be represented by an attorney.

Manor courts seem to have begun in the late 12thC, as a way for lords to supervise their tenants. However, written court records only really appear from the 1260s onwards. This was in response to pressure from above: legislation had prevented lords from forcing unfree tenants to attend manor courts and, at the same time, the royal courts were attracting more people with private legal business. The fact that these courts produced written records was one of the reasons for their popularity because it meant that judgements were recorded and stored centrally.[4] In order to compete, local landowners also began to keep a record of their manor courts in a systematic way. For the lords, it made sense to get as much business coming through their courts as possible, so they could profit from fees and penalties. For the tenants, the written record of proceedings meant that the court could provide evidence in disputes, as they could ask for past rolls to be examined. The fact that the earliest Dorking court roll to survive dates from 1282-3 is therefore not a surprise.

Where might the Dorking court have been held? At least sixty heads of household could be expected to turn up and, as informaiton was sometimes required of the whole assembly, they had to gather in a place where they could all participate. The 1649 map includes a piece of land called 'Court Close', which lay between the stream and the churchyard. It seems likely that this is equivalent to the small plot referred to as the 'Bertone' in the manorial documents of the 13th and 14th centuries. The name means a farmyard or land retained by the lord when the rest of the manor is let; it's derived from the Old English *bere-tun* or 'barley enclosure'. The Extent

---

[4] See Razi & Smith (1996).

doesn't specify what was grown on the Bertone in 1307 but it does say that the earl's barn was next to it. Perhaps the court was held in the barn when the weather was bad; alternatively, it might have been held in the church. Given that a clerk had to record everything in Latin on a parchment roll, it seems likely that proceedings were held indoors, once the written record had become an integral part of the system.

As we have seen, the steward presided over the court. In this, Dorking was a little behind the times as, from the 1260s onwards, reeves tended to take over this responsibility from stewards. A certain standard of behaviour among those attending was obviously enforced: in July 1283, Thomas de Bradele was held in contempt because he spoke badly of Gilbert Barnard in court. He was fined 6d.

The first piece of business at court was the hearing of 'essoins'. These were reasons for absence given on someone's behalf by a friend or neighbour who was at the court. Only three consecutive essoins were allowed before the absentee had to attend. Then the real business of the court began: general management of the manor, regulation of ale and bread sales, regulation of unfree 'villeins', private actions brought by individuals and, finally, some behaviour that might more properly be dealt with at the annual View of Frankpledge. There doesn't seem to have been an agenda as such, although, once a matter was raised and recorded, it tended to appear in the same position in each session until it was resolved.

Much of the business of the court rested on personal reputation rather than proof in the modern sense. For example, when Walter Semele and Avelina, his wife, brought a plea of trespass against Robert le Sutor, they could expect a certain process to take place. Walter and Avelina would have to present 'pledges': local people who volunteered to make sure everyone involved in the case followed the court's requests. Robert would first be 'attached' or summoned to appear at the next court. If he failed to appear, he would be 'distrained', some of his goods being confiscated to increase the pressure. When he did attend, the court might order a 'love day'. This was an opportunity for both parties to settle the matter out of court. If that didn't work, fines would be levied. In this case, Robert had obviously ignored the summons because, on the 17th September, he was distrained: a tanned hide was ordered to be confiscated. He was also bailed to appear without essoin by Adam de la Sonde, one of the pledges. The threat worked. At the following court, it was reported that both parties were in agreement and that Robert had been fined 6d.

As well as those directly involved, the reputation of those who stood as pledges was on the line. The same applied to any witnesses summoned to give evidence. For example, on the 26th October, Peter de la Rede produced witnesses to support certain charges which he had brought against William de Wadelshurst. Unfortunately for Peter, when they were questioned, his witnesses couldn't help. They said they knew nothing about about how or at what hour the alleged injury had taken place, except what Peter had told them. They obviously weren't prepared to perjure themselves in order to support a pal.

In 1282-3, most of the general manorial business related to timber being extracted without permission and to unauthorised grazing or hunting on the earl's land. Adam le Frend was cited for constantly breaking into the woods in Hambrech and carrying away timber from the middle of the wood without permission. He was fined 6d and had pledges provided by Nicholas de Westone and Ralph Opehulle. At the same November court, ten freeholders were fined for allowing their beasts to trespass in the earl's wood during the prohibited period; another five were bailed for the same offence and their pledges distrained to answer the charge. A further ten customary tenants, who all lived south of the Homwode, gave pledges which satisfied the court regarding damage to the earl's woods, while Gilbert de la Garstone was distrained for destruction of woods and for harbouring his son.

Several men were cited for hunting illegally, most notably Nicholas de Malemeyns. He was a knight who held Ockley manor. At the beginning of the 14thC, the king granted him the right to hold the assize of bread and ale and View of Frankpledge on his manor, as well as a market on Tuesdays and a fair on St Margaret's day. He also had 'free warren': the legal right to hunt small game on his own land. A glance at the map (p.81) shows that part of the manor of Ockley lay between the Brekesperes tenement and the Bere; perhaps this might account for Nicholas de Malemeyns straying so often out of his own warren and into the earl's. The matter was raised at every court session until the one held after Palm Sunday, when he gave pledges. Unfortunately, his pledges were not deemed good enough and were then summoned and fined for not providing the required surety. The matter dragged on throughout the year and we don't know what resolution was reached. De Malemeyns seems to have made something of a habit of hunting on other people's land, as similar pleas of trespass were brought by Thomas de Churchgate, Richard at Water and Nicholas de Westone, among others.

Some slightly less illustrious tenants were also cited for poaching. A jury of twelve of the manor's well-to-do freeholders swore on oath that William at Boxe was a wrongdoer in the earl's warren; he had to give four pledges of peace. Three other tenants (Ralph Dul, Gilbert Northbroc and Richard Tayleboys) made a similar accusation against twelve men who not only hunted but also sold the earl's rabbits. No fines or penalties are listed for any of these men, who included a member of the Sonde family and other wealthy freeholders such as Walter Alard, William Maynard and Richard de Weston. William Avrey was less lucky. he didn't defend himself against the accusation and was fined 6d.

The court roll for 1282-3 includes a number of private pleas, twenty-three of which were for trespass. Most don't contain any detail, apart from the names of those involved. However, the most long-running dispute occurred when Henry de Sutbury, a wealthy London merchant who owned 100 acres of land, complained that Sybil Brekespere and her sons cut down and damaged his wood at Garston and grazed their beasts on his meadow and pasture. He asked for £10 in damages and said he was ready to prove his case by jury. The subsequent inquiry proved that Sybil's sons often broke into de Sutbury's land at night and that Sybil approved of the grazing of their animals on his land. However, the jury said they didn't know how much damage was caused and the matter was held over to the next court. The issue wasn't mentioned again in the roll, so we don't know if de Sutbury received the outrageous sum he demanded.

Ten plaintiffs brought pleas of debt at the 1282-3 court, most of them against a single defendant (apart from the Prior of Reigate, who cited three people: Isabelle de Solaris, Thomas de Bradele and Margery de Kyngesfold, the latter both for unpaid rent). Unlike later court rolls, there is a fair bit of detail in some of these debt cases. For example, Alice at Wode brought a plea against John le White because she had loaned him 16d at Michaelmas two years previously, which he never paid back. He came to court and denied it; she dropped the charge and judgement was adjourned. One of the debt cases led to violence. John Kempe brought a charge against Agnes and Gilbert Barnard because he had loaned her a total of 5s 4½d. She not only didn't pay him back but he accused her of coming to his house and hitting him with a stone in his chest, so hard that he might have died. Her husband came to court to deny that she was either aggressive or dishonest and to refute the charge 'word for word'. As with so many cases in manor court rolls, we don't know the outcome. However, at the same time as John Kempe was bringing this charge against Agnes, there was an inquiry going on into the man himself for usury and treasure trove. Reading between the lines, it sounds as if John Kempe was a regular moneylender who had been informed on by one of his clients when she didn't want to pay him back.

Rabbits being chased by a ferret.

Trouble and Strife

An assault like the one allegedly carried out by Agnes Barnard on John Kempe would usually be dealt with through View of Frankpledge. This was a system, originating before the Conquest, whereby every man over the age of twelve had to belong to a tithing, which ensured his good behaviour. Each tithing had an elected headborough, who would levy any fines and report on the year's misdoings. By 1282, the yearly 'common fine' for Dorking had been fixed at 30s, plus any additional fines. In later years, the View took place during the week before the first session of the manorial court year, although in 1282 it occurred on the same day as the second manor court, held on the 5th October.

Two cases of violence were raised at this View. Firstly, it was presented that Maurice le Berde's wife had shed the blood of Nicholas le Wadel's wife; the assailant was ordered to attend a future court to answer the charge. Secondly, William Aguilun brought an action against William de la Bourne for badly beating and ill-treating his (Aguilun's) maidservant. De la Bourne had denied the charge, so it had gone before a jury which found him guilty.

These incidents were not the only acts of violence reported during the course of the court year. The same Gilbert Barnard mentioned above also got into trouble for threatening William, the rector of Bookham church, 'concerning his wife'. (Who knows what Agnes had been up to now?) In November, William Chaloner and Gilbert le Skinner were both accused of shedding blood. The case came up again the following February, when Gilbert defended himself against William, now named as the son of John le Chaloner. Gilbert was accused of coming into Dorking town and assaulting William: apparently, he swore at him, hit him and bit his finger. Another case involved a miller called John de London, who complained that William Berfot, a tanner, had hit him and drawn blood. Robert Deth was also charged with breaching the earl's peace to damages of 20s, which he denied.

During 1282-3, we learn some rather interesting details about one Gilbert Moraunt. He had obviously been cited for breaking the regulations regarding weights and measures but didn't appear at the second court of the year, his essoin being given by Thomas Sutor. At the same day's View of Frankpledge, a man called Adam le Rovere complained that he had been wrongfully arrested by Roger Clerk, servant of Hugh de Clare, and taken to the Dorking court. Roger had imprisoned Adam and bound him so tightly that the blood flowed, keeping him locked up between the hours of Prime and Vespers. Adam had previously been arrested and imprisoned at Guildford for the death of a William Pirie. However, he had been freed on licence and come back to Dorking because Richard Tayleboys and Agnes, widow Chapman, had agreed to give him two sheaves of corn at harvest. This was when he ran into Roger Clerk.

Two months later, Gilbert Moraunt was fined 2s for not presenting pledges at the manor court. In February, it was reported that his goods and chattels had been held and appraised by the coroner. (The only reason this came up in the manor court was because the coroner had then given them to Peter de la Dene, the headborough, who had passed them on to William de la Broke, who had delivered them elsewhere without a warrant or the presence of the earl's bailiffs.) It sounds very much like Gilbert Moraunt had fled the manor; perhaps someone warned him that Adam le Rovere had been freed from his imprisonment in Guildford. The reason for his concern becomes apparent when we consider the Surrey assize roll of 1293-4: Gilbert Moraunt was arrested for the death of William Purye of Dorking but found not guilty by the jury.[5]

Two men being put into the Tun, one resisting arrest.

---

[5] Bright (1884), p.54.

The Demesne

As well as running the manor court, Walter le Grant supervised the general business of the manor and farming of the demesne, both in Dorking and on a number of other manors, including Reigate and East Betchworth. However, the day to day management of each manor fell to a local reeve, assisted by two beadles. In Dorking, anyone who held a customary tenancy were required to serve as reeve 'if the lord wished'. Those who held half a virgate, a furlong or a cotland also had to serve as beadle 'if elected'. In return, their rent and services were remitted for the year and they would receive an allowance of grain for pottage (a thick soup or stew usually made from grain and vegetables).

During the 1282-3 court year, the reeve was a man called William about whom we know nothing further. His accounts don't survive, unlike those of Stephen Brouman, who was reeve in 1299-1300. Stephen held a furlong of land in the south of the manor, plus a field of free land. We don't have any further information about him, apart from the fact that he was personally unfree. However, we do know the names of some of his relatives. William Brouman was beadle in 1281-2; he was replaced by Richard Siward at the beginning of the 1282-3 court year. The same court roll also mentions a John Broman, who was ordered to take some vacant villein-land.

Chaucer, in his *Canterbury Tales*, was scathing about the reeve, describing him as cunning and deceitful, a terror to the tenants. Realistically, the role must have been a difficult and thankless one. The reeve had to run the manor for a year, from one Michaelmas (29th September) to the next. He was required to manage all aspects of farming on the lord's demesne, deciding what to plant and where to plant it, arranging the sale of produce and overseeing repairs to manorial buildings and equipment. He also had to collect the rents, fees and other payments that fell due during the year. As Bailey puts it in *The English Manor*, reeves "regularly made complex and sophisticated decisions about many aspects of demesne management, and it was often these dirty boot officials – rather than the lords or their stewards – who exhibited most commercial and farming acumen on seigneurial estates".[6] On some manors, this highly-responsible position was filled by a paid bailiff; in Dorking, it was a part-time role.

Unfortunately, Stephen's job as reeve was about to get more difficult. The year 1300 marks a turning point in England, when the economic expansion of the 13th century went into reverse. The ensuing recession saw rents and prices fall as demand dropped. This meant that standards of living rose for ordinary people but landlords fared less well.

Stephen would have kept detailed records, probably using tally sticks. His accounts had to be presented at the end of the manorial year but were audited at least once before their final acceptance. The accounts of 1299-1300 show this process in action: a number of Stephen's totals have been struck through and a new figure inserted. Manorial accounts don't show profit-and-loss in the modern way but set out receipts followed by expenses, which could include any payment the lord chose to make. The difference was carried over into the next year. The 'receipts' section could include payments that were owed but hadn't been collected; the reeve was held responsible for losses and could easily end up out of pocket at the end of his term. In 1300, the total receipts for Dorking were £139 19s 10¾d, including £32 11¼d carried over from the preceding year. Expenses totalled £102 8s 1¼d.

In *English Seigneurial Agriculture*, Campbell classifies the type of farming practised on Dorking's demesne land as "intensive cultivation with legumes", which he found was typical of Norfolk and Kent. He describes "similar advantages of deep and easily cultivated loam soils, a lack of institutional constraints, an abundance of cheap labour, an enterprising peasantry and ready access to major urban markets", all of which seem readily applicable to Dorking.[7] The best land on the manor lay to the north of the brook, where it consisted of good loam and chalk; this is where most of the demesne fields lay. To the south, the soil was a heavy clay, which the slightest drop of rain turned into a quagmire. During 1299-1300, Stephen planted wheat, oats and barley. He tried to combat the clay soil by marling

---

[6] Bailey (2002), p.99.
[7] Campbell (2000), p.290.

the fields, probably sourcing the chalk from Dorking Downs and Summerleas.[8] The manor had a special cart for the purpose.

According to the Extent, the earl's demesne consisted of over 200 acres available for arable, at least 30 acres of pasture, 12 acres of meadow and more than 230 acres of woodland. As well as wheat, oats and barley, fields could be planted with vetch, a legume which restores nitrogen content in the soil and can help to choke weed growth when sown between grain crops. It could also be used to feed ewes and lambs at the end of winter. These crops were planted at the Betine, Parrok, Mapeldrefeld and Shiplond, all located in the best land north of the brook, and at the Lese, which lies to the southwest of the town. Bray's notes on the Extent make it clear that the crops were sown in rotation. 11 acres at the Parrok could be sown with alternate crops over two years and then had to lie fallow in the third, while the remaining 20 acres could be sown every year. Shiplond, Mapledrefeld and two acres of the Lese were available for wheat, then oats, then lying fallow, while the main part of the Lese (36½ acres) could only be sown every seventh year to improve the pasture. There was also land which could be sown in the seventh year and then for the following three years: 12 acres at Bernfelde, 40 acres at Eldendene and 30 acres at Middelinnome.

The customary tenants were required to provide labour services to help till the demesne fields. How much they did depended on how much land they held. The work began after Michaelmas, when all the virgaters and ferlingsmen had to bring their own carts and oxen in order to transport and spread manure on the earl's fields. The next task was to sow wheat and oat seed, which took place twice a year, in the winter and during Lent. Only a fraction of the demesne land was worked by the tenants: 13 acres 1 rod of land were sown in winter, when the virgaters and ferlingsmen had to plough and harrow the soil and thresh the seed for sowing. Virgaters had to work one acre each, seven of the half-virgaters half an acre and the rest of the half-virgaters and ferlingsmen one rod. In spring, 13 acres 2½ rods had to be ploughed on the same basis and then everyone came for a day and a half to harrow in preparation for sowing oat seed. Each tenant brought his

---

[8] Chalk was taken from these fields, according to the 1649 survey.

or her own horse to do so and, on the full day, received a meal provided by the earl. Additionally, another 13 acres 2 rods of fallow land had to be ploughed. Obviously, this doesn't add up to anything like the 200 acres that could be planted with arable crops and the earl had full-time staff to work the rest of his land. There was a ploughman and a man to drive the plough, who received 5s and 6s per annum respectively, and a harrower.

Once the crop was growing, it had to be hoed to keep down the weeds. Again, all the virgaters and ferlingsmen were expected to hoe a certain number of acres: four for a virgater and two for everyone else. Then, at harvest-time, the customary tenants were joined by the cottars, who reaped and bound the corn for five weeks over 36 acres 1 rod of land. This work began on Lammasday (1st August). Two cottars (Robert at Bere and William Renger) also owed an additional acre or half-acre respectively of reaping and binding. Finally, the virgaters and ferlingsmen had to spend a day carrying the corn to the earl's barn. There is no evidence of week-work being expected of Dorking tenants (although two cottars on East Betchworth manor did have to turn up twice a week to complete 176 'small jobs' in 1299-1300).

Medieval farming was a mixture of arable and livestock. By the end of the 1299-1300 accounting year, Stephen's store account included twenty-one pigs, one draught animal, two mares, a colt, twenty-four bullocks and four cows. Murrain (an infectious disease that plagued medieval farms) had carried off two draught animals, three mares, three bullocks and two pigs. Pasture for grazing was scattered throughout the manor at the Innome, the Hambrech, the Lese and Burnhaldret, supplemented by land at Redlevet

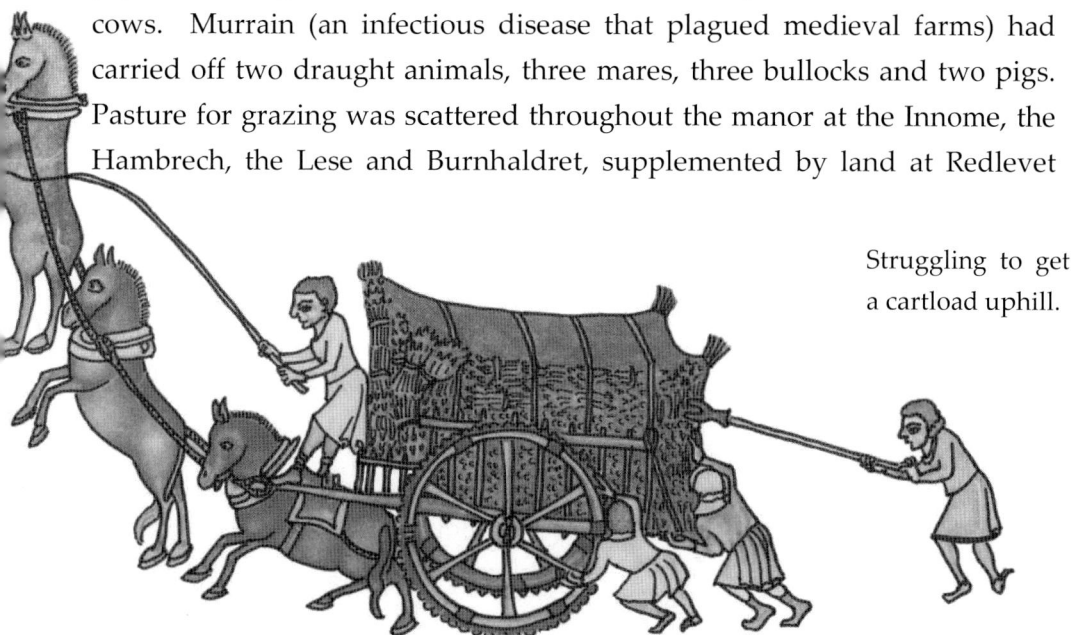

Struggling to get a cartload uphill.

(just south of the town) and at Brokwick, Byllynggesmor, Lobbesmor and Winchescumesmor (further south and west). Pasture could also be a source of income, being leased to other people so they could graze their animals. In 1299-1300, £1 14s was raised in this way. A swineherd was employed to watch the earl's pigs when they were in the Homwode during the autumn and Stephen's accounts also include the cost of hogwash in the winter.

Fencing was needed to enclose the fields where livestock was grazing. The customary tenants had to provide hurdles for the purpose in three parts of the demesne: the Bertone, the Lese and Mapeldrefeld. Tenants who held a virgate were required to enclose four perches of land at the Lese, providing two hurdles each. Half-virgaters had to supply one hurdle and ferlingsmen half a hurdle, enclosing two perches and half a perch respectively. Most of the half-virgaters had to enclose at the Lese, which lies on the western edge of the manor, but John de Proteriche supplied his hurdle at the Bertone, the small croft next to the earl's barn. Five of the ferlingsmen also enclosed at the Bertone, while all the customary tenants had to help enclose Mapeldrefeld, on the northernmost edge of the manor. Gates were known as 'hatches' and were the responsibility of the landholder. In 1299-1300, a new gate was made for the Lese, as a cost of 15d for the carpenter's labour.

Livestock also had to be fed during the winter. The earl's meadows were at Burnemed, Hamsted, Medmulle and Redmed. For the tenants, this meant that eight acres split into three pieces had to be mown and the hay gathered by the virgaters and ferlingsmen. It was the cottars' job to rake the hay as it was collected, transport it to the barn door and then stack it. The division into three pieces may be because the meadows were scattered through the manor: Hamsted and the Medmulle lie next to the North Brook, while Burnemed and Redmed are much further south, the former next to the Homwode, the latter next to the Lese. Corn was also bought in the year 1299-1300, presumably as additional animal feed.

Woodland formed about half of the demesne, a notably high proportion. The Homwode was the most important, supplemented by 116 acres at Brokwick, 60 acres at Ashcombe and smaller stretches of timber at

Burnhaldret, Hambrech and the Lese.[9] Medieval woodland comprised 'standard' trees left to grow tall and surrounded by coppiced 'stools' producing poles which could be regularly harvested at anything up to ten years. The resource had to be carefully managed by a forester or 'wodeward'; in 1299-1300, this was a man called William de la Dene. All customary tenants were expected to help transport firewood ('talwode') from Dorking to Kingston: one cartload (50 talsides) by a virgater, half a cartload (25 talsides) by half-virgaters and thirteen talsides by the ferlingsmen. This was a lucrative business for the earl. In 1300, the population of London was about 80,000 and the consumption of fuel for industrial and domestic purposes was relentless. The price of firewood had gone up sharply in the later 13th century and the city was supplied from a number of manors within a nineteen mile radius, in the form of charcoal, faggots or talwode. Kingston was a key staging post, where woodmongers hired boats from local men and shipped both firewood and building timber down to London.[10]

Another of the earl's paid employees was the warrener. He lived in a lodge overlooking the earl's warren, where rabbits were bred for consumption, gifts or sale. He also supervised the hunting available to the earl in his park. Although the accounts of 1299-1300 do not mention any sales of rabbits, they were definitely present on the manor, both as a temptation and a nuisance. As we have seen, the 1282-3 court roll names thirteen men accused of poaching and selling the earl's rabbits, while the Extent says that six acres of land at Shiplond couldn't be sown with crops because of them.

Running a manor entailed expenses. In 1299-1300, these included plough expenses, cart expenses, mill expenses and repairs to the barn and ox-shed. Iron and steel were bought for repairing the plough, in consultation with the smith, as well as a new ploughshare and cultor and horseshoes for harrowing. The wood cart required repairs to the wheels, involving 'trundle-wheels' and four clouts with nails. (A clout was a metal plate used for repairs.) Clouts were also needed for the marl cart and grease was

---

[9] Figures from the 16thC copy of the Extent.
[10] See Galloway et al (1996).

bought for both vehicles. There was a Richard le Smyth in Dorking in this period, so perhaps he was the man who did this work. His smithy may have been located on the corner of the high street and Mill Lane.[11]

Only 7d was spent on tiling and repairs for the barn, ox-shed and 'hay-house', the work being done as piece-work (hired labour). However, the customary tenants all owed labour-services for such repairs, so it may be that there was work done that year that didn't appear in the accounts. The big spend was on repairs to both the mills. Unfortunately, this section of the accounts is damaged but it was obviously a major undertaking. For the Estmell (east mill), a new millstone was brought from Kingston and steel bought to pierce it.[12] 100 boards and 500 nails were purchased for the mill beam and the water-wheel was mended as piece-work. The mill-pond was cleaned and the top of the beam fastened against something called the 'thullyeng'. All this was undertaken by command of Walter le Bacheler, the earl's steward in that year, and supervised by Robert Carpenter of Betchworth. At the Medmell (middle mill), a new waterwheel, an 'oggesweyel' and a 'fissebed' were made, again by piece-work.[13] 175 feet of

A thatched mill, with eel and fish traps upstream of the millrace.

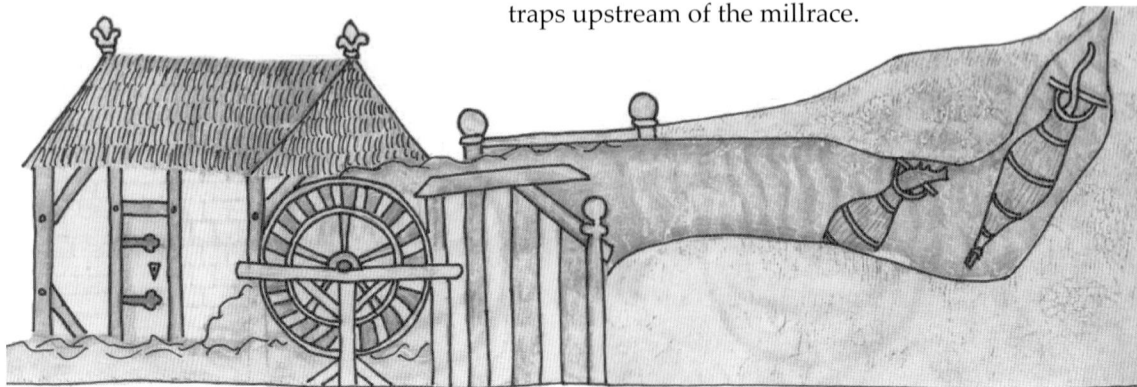

---

[11] See DM R734.

[12] The East Betchworth accounts for the same year put the cost of a new millstone at £3, plus 6d to convey it from where it was bought, 1d for wharfage, 4d for wine for the seller, 16d to transport it upstream to Kingston and 9d for unloading from the boat and onto a waggon.

[13] 'Thullyng' may mean a wooden post. 'Oggesweyel' may be something to do with eels and 'fissebed' with fish; perhaps these were traps to prevent them getting into the mill-race?

sawn planks, 200 nails and steel for a set of spindles were also bought. All this was expensive: £7 1½d was spent in total on the two mills.

Walter was the brother of Nicholas le Bacheler, who also held some official role in the earl's household. Both men witnessed a number of contemporary property deeds and Walter acted as a pledge in several manorial court cases.[14] Another official who appeared in the accounts was the earl's chaplain, named as Sir Oliver (the honorific was given to priests as well as knights in this period). He received livery of £9 14s 7d. The beadles of Dorking are not named in the accounts, although William Renger might have been one of them: he had tallies regarding mill and market profits against his name but the entry was then crossed out. Other reeves are named, such as Nicholas de Santon, reeve of Reigate, and John at Wode, reeve of East Betchworth, with whom Stephen Brouman must have worked closely.

Agriculture and husbandry were not the only source of income for the earl. As well as rent, customary tenants owed other payments. When a tenant died, his heirs had to pay 'heriot'. This was an Anglo-Saxon custom; originally it signified the weapons that a warrior had received from his lord but, by the later medieval period, it meant the deceased's best beast. Heriot, along with the 'entry fine' due to the earl when a tenant's heir took over his land, meant that death duties could be rather steep. The earl also received a payment when freehold land was transferred. The new freeholder had to a pay a relief (Lat *relevium*) to the lord and swear fealty, while the transfer of title would be recorded in a written deed. A freeholder might also have to pay a quitrent, in lieu of any services that were still attached to the piece of land in question.

The earl also collected 'Romescot', a payment to the church at Rome which consisted of one penny from a married man and a halfpenny from a single man or woman. This was a special English offering of long-standing. Initially, various Anglo-Saxon kings had made ad-hoc gifts to the Pope to show their devotion to the Holy See but, by the late Anglo-Saxon period, this had become an annual donation to which every adult man and woman

---

[14] BL 9016, 18571, 18597, 18603, 18616 for Nicholas; BL 9011, 9012 and 18612 for Walter.

contributed. In 1299-1300, 4s 7d was collected from the Dorking customary tenants; as 3s was passed to the church each year, the earl made a small profit. There was also 'tallage', a tax levied at the discretion of the earl and much resented. By this period, the Dorking tally had become fixed at £4 a year in total.

The manor court brought in a tidy sum for the earl in various fines and penalties and he received at least 30s a year from the View of Frankpledge. The earl also received 'pannage', the payment made by the tenants in return for the earl allowing their pigs to forage in the Homwode after Martinmas (11th November). It was levied at a penny a pig, although in the Extent the assumption was made that all tenants should pay, regardless of whether they used it or not.

The customary tenants also owed 'mill soke', the requirement to grind their own corn at the earl's mill and have a toll exacted by the miller. As we have seen, the earl had two watermills in Dorking, both of which were usually 'farmed': someone took them over for a fixed sum and then kept whatever profits he made beyond that amount. In 1299, William de la Strode paid £22 13d, a sum which probably included the 'farm' of the twice-weekly market.[15] Chaucer was just as scathing about the miller as he was about the reeve, describing him as a thief of corn who charged at three-times the going rate. There was obviously some dispute in 1282, as six tenants attended court and put it to the miller that they had performed mill soke; the miller came and said that they had, so they were acquitted. Their names were Gilbert at Broke, Robert Bronild, Ralph de Fernore, Alice at Rugge, Roger at Rugge and Robert de Upbrok. The earl also received the 'third penny' from tolls paid in Guildford, which brought in a fixed amount of 40s.[16] It's not clear why this was included in the Dorking accounts.

As well as payments in coin, the earl received payments in kind. Stephen Brouman's store account for 1299-1300 included 93 hens and 415 eggs, received from the customary tenants as part of their rent, plus six capons,

---

[15] Although not specified in the 1299-1300 accounts, the mills and market were usually farmed together. The Extent states that the two watermills were worth £11 11s 8d and the twice-weekly market and annual fair were worth £12.
[16] Granted to the earl by Henry III (Brayley (1841), p.78).

four sticks of eels, one pair of gilded spurs, 1lb of cumin and 2lb of pepper. The gilded spurs were paid as rent for one of the two properties held by knight's fee: Bonets and Chert. (It's not known why only one of these properties had produced rent that year.) The capons, eels and spices were annual quitrents; a 'stick' consisted of 25 dried or smoked eels but we don't know who paid them, as they disappear from the record after 1300. Only the cumin can be linked to a particular property: half an acre of land in the Shiplond which, at about this time, was granted by Richard de la Sonde to Roger de la Sonde. The cumin was to be paid at Whitsun 'for all customary service'.[17] Payment in spices was not unusual. They were widely available in this period and easily obtained, even in rural areas. A grocer was known as an 'espicer' and sold imported cloves, mace, ginger, cinnamon and saffron, as well as pepper and cumin. Even the ordinary shopper might buy a few ounces for medicinal use or to flavour his or her food; cumin in particular was used as a stimulant for appetite and a digestif after a meal, as well as to treat a variety of ailments from the common cold to toothache.[18] One of Dorking's freeholders was called Gilbert le Spicer. His property lay west of the Homwode, next to the Hambrech, and it may well have been he who supplied the pepper and the cumin that ended up in the earl's store.

Catching partridges in a net.

[17] BL 18571.
[18] See Francia (2011).

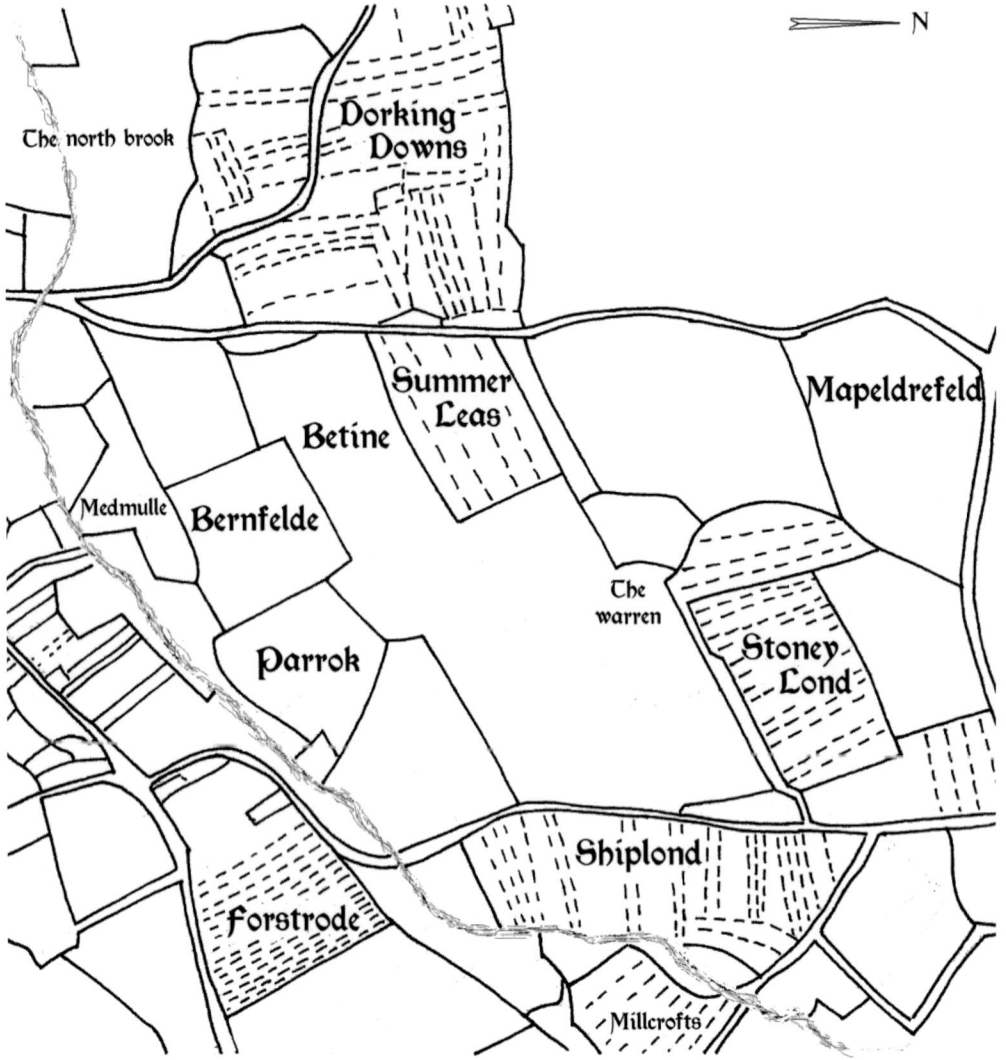

A plan of the demesne land and common fields.

Who Lived on the Manor?

As mentioned previously, two properties on Dorking manor were held by knight's fee. In 1307, the larger of the two (a virgate) was held by Robert Bonet and the smaller half-virgate by the son of Richard at Chert. As well as making an annual payment of a pair of gilded spurs, they were each expected to attend the manor court. Robert Bonet seems to have found the latter particularly inconvenient: he was essoined eight times during the 1282-3 court year.[19] The only information we have about Richard at Chert suggests that he had some dealings with the City; in 1294, he owed £4 10s to William Bernard, a citizen of London.[20]

Socially, these men would have been at the top of the local tree, alongside many of the freeholders who held their property by deed rather than customary service. The size of freehold plots on the manor varied widely. As we have seen, a hundred acres belonged to Henry de Sutbury, the wealthy London merchant. It was subsequently inherited by his son-in-law, Clerekyn de Florence, and was still known as 'Subberies' (a corruption of 'Sutbury') in the 17thC. The land seems to have been alienated (sold outright) by the earl, presumably to raise money. This was probably investment property, producing an income for the Sutburys. We don't know how often Henry visited his Dorking land but, when he appears in the court roll, it seems to be in person rather than through an attorney. Perhaps he was a regular visitor.

Several other large freehold properties can be identified on the map, notably those held by the Ashcombes and by Maurice de Ewekene, as well as the significant amount of land amassed by the Sonde family near Bury Hill. Other freehold properties were smaller, such as those held by Robert Deth, Gilbert at Houke or Peter Isemonger. Thomas Gegge was beadle of Reigate in 1282; perhaps the property called 'Gages' was held by him or a member of his family. One person might hold multiple properties. For instance, Walter le Mum, another merchant active in London, held a tenement, two messuages, two curtilages and a croft, plus an acre and a rod

---

[19] It has been suggested that he was working for the earl (Day & Ettlinger (2015), p.4).

[20] PRO C 241/27/111.

of land, but his name only appears on the map at 'Mumms mead', near the brook.

Some freeholders also rented large amounts of customary land from the earl. William Belde, Thomas le Rede and William de Wynterfold all had 300 acres 'held in villeinage'. This meant that they were personally free but owed all the dues and services connected with that piece of land. Gilbert at Felde, Roger at Monte and John Pouk held twenty acres on the same terms, while Edward de Garston rented forty acres in the Lese. Occasionally, land was transferred when it shouldn't have been. One piece of villein land came under scrutiny at the manor court because it had been granted by Richard Doul to Gilbert Doul. Gilbert seems not to have known that the land could not legally be transferred; he swore to that effect at court and the land was taken back into the earl's hand.

The Dorking property market was flourishing, as can be seen from a number of surviving deeds and the information presented in the Extent. Most of this activity was focussed on messuages, curtilages, shops and small acreages in or near the town. (A 'messuage' was the building or buildings on a plot known as a 'curtilage'.) Thomas at Churchgate was particularly noteworthy in this regard: he amassed a large number of properties, from a messuage received from his father to a meadow he got from Peter Wyleman, a curtilage from Richard Tayleboys and an acre of land from Edward le Mum, among others. Thomas appears in the 1282-3 court roll as a brewer. He witnessed several property deeds at around that time and served on a manorial jury investigating the poaching of the earl's rabbits. We don't know why he was so active in the Dorking property market. Some freeholders held one or more shops, including Simon le Carpenter, Walter Harm, Walter de Lustreforde, Agnes, widow of Robert Page and Matilda, daughter of William de le Priest.[21]

Freeholders had tenants of their own, paying them rent. For example, a man called John Togod lived in a messuage for which he paid 1d per annum. When his landlord, Peter, son of Elmer de Newdigate, granted the messuage to William, son of Walter de la Sonde of Dorking, the deed

---

[21] This may be the same man as the cottar named as 'William le Pris' in the Extent.

included Togod's 'entire right and homage', plus the penny rent.[22]   We know nothing more about John Togod but he was obviously local as he is described as 'of Dorking'. This provides a salutary reminder that not everyone who lived in the town appears in the manorial documents which provide most of our information. In another example, Walter le Mum leased a messuage and curtilage on Suthestret to someone called William le Comber for 2s per annum. It lay between the properties of Thomas le 'Fuzel' and Simon le Rede and backed on to land held by Richard Tailleboys. By 1311, when Walter gave the 2s annual rent to Robert de la Sonde and his wife, Simon le Rede was still in possession but the other two nearby properties were held by Peter le 'Foghel' and Alice Tailleboys.[23]

Of the surviving deeds from this period, only one can be matched precisely with the information set out in the Extent. In it, Henry Oslak gave to Emma, daughter of Ralph le Rede, a certain acre of land near to the King's Highway from Dorking to Reigate. She paid ten shillings and had to perform the annual service due by law and custom to the earl. The deed was sealed by Henry Oslak and witnessed by William Aguilon, Walter Alard, Ralph de la Chert, Richard de la Chert, Thomas at Churchgate, William Maynard, Walter le Mum, Robert de la Sonde, Nicholas de Weston and others.[24]

Several religious orders held land in Dorking. The Knights Templar had a house on the high street, granted to them by the fifth earl, along with the services of his man, Pagan Wrang.[25]   The Templars held the property until their suppression in 1312, when it was transferred to the Knights of St John; it was subsequently known as the 'Cross House'. The Priory of Kilburn held the nearby manor of Milton and the prioress was repeatedly cited for not attending the Dorking manor court.[26]   Finally, two surviving deeds

---

[22] BL 18557.

[23] BL 9015 and 18603.

[24] BL 18581. See also BL 9002 and 9017.

[25] There is some dispute about the date but it must have been before Earl William's death in May 1240. Pagan Wrang was subsequently accused of the murder of a chaplain in the building but died before it came to court (Bright (1884), pp.53-4).

[26] The priory must have held land on Dorking manor. In the 1380s, the prioress was frequently summoned regarding land called Snokeshull.

refer to the hide of land called 'Hamstede', which had formerly belonged to the Priory of Holy Trinity, London.[27]

Roughly half the residents of the manor lived on the thirty-eight customary tenancies. In addition, seventeen cottars held a cotland or, in two cases, half a cotland. This tallies with the Dorking entry in Domesday Book, which records thirty-eight *villani* and thirteen *bordarii*. Three of the customary holdings comprised a whole virgate of land. In 1307, two of these were held by Hugh de la Pleystowe and William de Langshete, while the third was referred to as the 'land of Wadelshurst'. A glance at the map (pp.80-1) shows that the Langshete tenement lay next to the Bere, while Pleystowe and Wadelshurst lay in the south of the manor, with Wadelshurst bordering Sussex. Each virgater paid rent of £1 16s per annum and had to give the earl two hens at Christmas and twenty eggs at Easter.

As we have already seen, the customary tenants had to provide a significant number of payments and services to the earl. These fell due at different times during the year. Beginning with the Christmas hens, there followed the winter ploughing in January, the first third of their rent in February (at Candlemas on the 2nd), spring ploughing during Lent and the delivery of eggs at Easter. Monday or Tuesday in the second week after Easter was Hokeday, when the tenants had to supply hurdles, followed by the second rent payment due at Whitsun (the seventh Sunday after Easter). The 1st of August was Lammasday, traditionally the first day of harvest and

Two men ploughing with oxen.

---

[27] BL 9000 & BL 18563.

also when Romescot had to be paid. This was followed by the third rent payment at Michaelmas (29th September) and, finally, the tallage tax was due at All Saints (1st November). The burdens on the earl's tenants were not light.

In addition, they were expected to help repair the earl's barn and ox-shed and to provide carrying-service for the earl with horse and pack within and without the County of Surrey, for which they would receive allowances of food and ale. In 1282-3, ten tenants were fined at the manor court because they had been summoned to cart stone from Horsham to Reigate and hadn't turned up (despite promising they would).[28]

The names of those described in the Extent as holding customary tenancies became associated with their plots for centuries to come, probably because this document served as a fixed point in the administration of the manor. The names were marked on the 1649 map, so we have some idea where most of these tenants lived. As their 'surnames' will recur throughout this book, it seems useful to list those named in 1307. Nineteen of the customary tenancies were half a virgate in size and were tenanted by the following people:

Henry Brekespere	John de Proteriche
Walter Brekespere	John at Risbrugge
Richard de Brugesulle	Robert at Rugge
William de Brugesulle	Roger at Rugge
Agnes at Grenehurst	Alice at Russete
Richard at Helde	Richard Sprot
Walter at Hulle	Walter Stel
Adam de Langshete	Thomas Tayllur
Robert de Langshete	Richard de Upbroke
Robert at Pleystowe	

---

[28] Perhaps unsurprisingly, one was Sibil, widow Brekespere. The others were: Robert Bronild, William de Brugesulle, jnr, William de Brugesulle, snr, Gilbert de la Broke, Adam Langshete, Robert de Pleystowe, Odo le Rede, Roger at Rugge and Richard Siward.

Their rent ranged from 11s 3d to £1 2s 6d per annum, presumably depending on the quality of the land. Although the payments and services were less onerous than for a virgater, they fell due just the same throughout the year. All the half-virgaters lived south of the Homwode, apart from John de Proteriche. All apart from Walter Stel can easily be located on the map; it may be that he lived at the tenancy later known as 'Arnolds'.

The fact that we can precisely locate many of these plots allows us to get some idea of which of these tenants were neighbours. This is sometimes supported by other evidence. For instance, the Brekesperes and the Brugesulles lived on adjoining properties. That the families were somewhat intertwined is apparent from the manor court roll of 1282-3, when a question of inheritance took up quite a bit of time. It seems that William Brekespere and William de Brugesulle had both died before the court year began. On his deathbed, William Brekespere had apparently given a bronze pot to Sybil, his brother's widow, and there had been an inquiry into this matter. Another inquiry was then conducted by six jurymen into other goods belonging to him which had come into the hands of the late William de Brugesulle. The latter had obviously made a will: his executors were required to answer to Walter Brekespere regarding certain debts. It was judged that Walter should receive the value of the contested goods (a total of 10s 9½d) from the younger William de Brugesulle, who was one of the executors. (As an added complication, Henry, the chaplain of Capel was named as executor but he denied the role and was eventually let off the hook by the younger William.) Without wishing to be unkind but taking into account other information that survives regarding the redoutable widow, the suspicion occurs that Sybil may not have been given the bronze pot so much as taken it. She was in trouble that year for unpaid rent to the tune of 10s 6d, for unlawful possession of 6d alms from the earl and for breaking into his park. Her feud with Henry de Sutbury reveals that her sons were called Gilbert and Henry.

Sixteen tenants held a furlong or, in two cases, half a furlong of land.

In 1307, their names were:

Robert at Bourne	Alice, widow of Richard at Hacche
Stephen Brouman	Gilbert at Holoweye
Richard at Cherche	Alice at Lyth
Walter at Clerhole	Maurice at Lyth
William le Clerk	John at Mesbroke
Peter at Dene	Agnes Milward
Peter Godard	William le Sket
Matilda Godwyne	William Thurbarn

Their rents varied between 5s 7½d and 18s per annum, apart from Agnes Milward and Alice, the widow, who held half a furlong each and paid 4s 6d. They also gave half a hen at Christmas and 2½ eggs at Easter (how one paid half a hen or half an egg will become clear later). Most of these tenancies lay south of the Homwode. One of these plots was later known as 'Kitlands' and it may be that Agnes Milward lived there. We can pinpoint where the rest of the ferlingsmen lived by their names.

Five of them were required to supply hurdles at the Bertone: Robert at Bourne, Peter at Dene, Peter Godard, Matilda Godwyne and William le Clerk. It seems logical that their plots would be nearest to the town but that's not necessarily the case. Bourne's and Godwyne's lay north of the Homwode but so too did the Holoweye and Gilbert at Holoweye had to enclose at the Lese. Likewise, if William le Clerk held any of the land later known as 'Clerks', then why did he have to enclose at the Bertone? We don't know precisely where Peter at Dene or Peter Godard lived, so can't explore this any further.

Feeding chicks. Mother hen not to scale.

On the bottom rung of the social ladder were the cottars. These were the poorest of the earl's tenants, holding a cotland or even half a cotland. In 1307, their names were:

Richard at Bere	Roger Osward
Matilda, widow of William Bynorthebroke	William Osward
Matilda de la Claygate	William le Pris
Odo at Dene	William le Rede
Thomas at Dene	William Renger
Walter le Dighere	Ralph le Stull
Richard le Doule	Clarisse Sweteriche
John Fody	Adam Tailleboye
Cote Gerdilde	

Apart from in the Extent, few of the cottars appear in the manorial documents. When they do, it's usually to do with the inheritance of their cotland. Inheritance on Dorking manor was governed by the practice known as 'Borough English', where the youngest son inherited everything (rather than the eldest), followed by the youngest daughter if no son were available. Although this is frequently described as an Anglo-Saxon custom, in fact it was a post-Conquest development: the term was coined in Nottingham when a court case of 1327 drew the attention of lawyers to the fact that inheritance practices differed in the French and English boroughs of the town.[29] 'Borough English' was particularly practised in Surrey, Sussex and Norfolk, which makes one wonder whether it was a custom imposed by the de Warennes on their tenants. Be that as it may, when a Dorking tenant died, his heir had to come to the court, pay the heriot and entry fine and swear fealty to the earl. Although the earl could grant the land elsewhere, in reality inheritance was assured unless there was good reason not to allow it.

Sometimes the heir refused to take the land. In January 1282/3, it was reported that Adam Renger was dead and his son, William, was named as

---

[29] See Corner (1855). There is no evidence of 'Borough English' in Anglo-Saxon England.

the next heir by everyone at the manor court. Their cotland can't have been very profitable as no heriot was paid and William obviously said he didn't want it. At the following court, the reeve was ordered to get 3s for the tenement if he could find someone who was willing to take it. In the end, William came and paid the entry fine; his pledges, Richard Harm and William Osward, confirmed that he would keep the property in good order. Another cotland that came to the court's attention that year was that of the late Geoffrey de la Dene. His widow, Gufra, undertook to deal with it justly but their daughter, Alice, claimed part of the tenement as her right and the matter was postponed until the next court. Gufra then paid 4s to hold the land until her son, Thomas, came of age, plus 2s for Geoffrey's heriot.[30] Her pledges were Peter at Hambreche and Peter at Dene.

Four cotlands were identified by name in the 1649 survey: 'Coillards' and 'Ringers' at either end of East Street, 'The Stockhouse' on West Street and 'North Brook' between the Medmulle and a lane running alongside the demesne land. Others were named in the late 14th and early 15th century court rolls as 'Alotislond', 'Brokeres', 'Cokerelles', 'Fothieslond', 'Fusties' and 'Prysildelond'. Perhaps the most poignant is that of Clarisse Sweteriche, whose cottage was still being named as 'formerly Claricie Sweteriche' in the 1380s. She only held half a cotland in 1307 and nothing more is known about her but she found a kind of immortality thereafter.

These were small plots, not large enough to support a family, so those who lived on them must have hired out their labour. They also held pieces of land scattered throughout the 'common fields'. Presumably, these had originally been worked jointly by all the tenants but there is no evidence in the surviving manorial documents for the organisation of such communal work. The common fields lay primarily to the north-east of the town and were called Shiplond, Stoneylond, Forstrode, Dorking Downs and Summerleas.[31] South of Eststret lay the 'Bovetoune' fields ('above-the-

---

[30] The roll says 'Alice, widow of Geoffrey at Dene' but this seems to be a clerical error.
[31] Dorking Downs may also have been known as 'North Down'. BL 9019 refers to a common field called 'Le Nouhtdone', an acre of which was surrounded by church land.

town') and there also seems to have been some common land up at Bury Hill. Each cotland included varying amounts of land in these fields. To give an example, in 1571 the Rengers tenement was recorded as being 7 acres 1 rod in total: one acre at Bury Hill, one and a half acres and one rod at Dorking Downs, one acre at Stoneylond, three rods at Shiplond, three rods at Hidefeld, one acre at Mylcroft and half an acre each on the east and west sides of the Forstrode.

By the early 14thC, some of this land was already in private hands. As we have seen, half an acre in the Shiplond was held by the Sonde family, for which they supplied a pound of cumin in lieu of customary service. The Bovetoune plots seem to have been the earliest to go, as the holdings were gradually surrendered to people with property on the south side of Eststret. Land in the common fields could also be leased out, although it needed the earl's permission (as the Douls discovered to their cost). In 1307, Henry at Hethe's land included half an acre in Stoneylond and, in the 1340s, two tenants surnamed Clerk and Bythenorthbroke leased out their half acres in the same place. However, Cotmandene seems to have remained common land, where the cottars (or cotmen) could graze their animals and where the Ascension Day fair was held.[32]

Two plots of land called Claygate and Oswards lay southwest of the town, at each end of a lane to the Homwode. They seem rather large to be cotlands, as does Trasshes, a tenement on the other side of Godwyns which was described as a cotland in the 1381-2 court roll. Perhaps the original thirteen cotlands in the town and at the Bere were subsequently added to, resulting in the seventeen listed in the Extent.

Richard at Bere's was the only cotland in Waldeborough, where he paid 9s per annum in rent. He didn't owe any hens and eggs because it was his job to collect them, in the company of the beadle of Walde, and then bring them to the town. Another role attached to the Bere cotland was to collect all the heriot that fell due and bring the beasts to the earl's store. Richard also had to work with the reeve to collect other customary payments. If someone were arrested in Waldeborough during daylight hours, it was his

---

[32] It was certainly held there by 1649.

job to bring them to Dorking; if at night, he had to keep the miscreant at his house until the morning. Other than that, he owed the same dues and services as the other cottars. Richard only appears once in the court roll for 1282-3, when he gave an essoin for Maurice de Ewekene, whose property lay not far from the Bere.

The rest of the cottars had to provide two hens (one for a half-cottage), plus five eggs (or 2½). As well as their agricultural services and carrying-service, the male cottars also had to serve as beadle if elected and to take anyone arrested in the Liberty of Dorking to Guildford for judgement or to the Dorking Tun until the reeve could deal with the matter. If the malefactor escaped, any cottar had to help the beadle to recapture him or her. Most of the cotlands were held on these terms, paying 6s rent per annum. An exception was that of William le Rede: although his cottage was a whole one, not a half, he owed one hen and 2½ eggs. He also paid a halfpenny Romescot, which suggests that he was single. Otherwise, his services were the same as the other cottars.

The cottars traditionally received a meal on Christmas Day provided by the earl, which conjures up a pleasant vision of feasting at Reigate castle. However, the accounts of 1299-1300 refer to 21d spent on pottage on Christmas Day for fourteen cottars. This creates a bit of a puzzle. Although, according to Bray's notes, the Extent specifies that all the half-virgaters, ferlingsmen and cottars should receive a Christmas meal worth 1½d (apart from Wiliam le Rede who only received three farthings), the manorial accounts from 1329-30 onwards consistently include the 'money paid to thirteen cottars for that Christmas meal which they are owed as custom'. As Domesday Book tells us that there were thirteen 'bordars' living in the manor in the mid-eleventh century, it seems likely that those living on the original thirteen cotlands received the Christmas Day meal. Perhaps the clerk who drew up the original Extent made a mistake in assuming the earl's largesse was more widely spread (or perhaps Bray made a transcription error in his notes).

It might seem obvious that those people who held customary tenancies were personally unfree but that is not necessarily the case. The services associated with such a tenancy would be owed by anyone who took on the land, regardless of their personal status. Throughout the manorial records, a distinction is drawn between those who were 'unfree tenants' (Lat *tenente nativi*) and those who were 'unfree of the lord' (Lat *nativi domini*) or 'unfree of the earl' (Lat *nativi comiti*). Two payments were used in medieval law to indicate unfree status: 'chevage' (for permission to leave the manor) and 'merchet' (for permission to marry). Unfortunately, there is no record of anyone paying chevage in the 1282-3 court roll, while the accounts of 1299-1300 include two ploughshares paid as chevage without specifying by whom. Only one example of merchet can be found, when Richard de Brugesulle gave 12d for permission for one of his daughters to wed. Confusingly, in the Extent, the virgaters and ferlingsmen are described as owing merchet but not the cottars. This seems a little strange but may be because merchet tended to be paid by the more well-to-do 'villeins'.[33]

It may be that all the Dorking customary tenants named in the Extent were personally unfree but the only way we can be sure is if they are specifically identified as such in the manorial records. As we have seen, Richard de Brugesulle paid merchet, so we know he was a 'villein'. At the November court, Odo de la Dene was offered a piece of land by the earl and, when he refused to take it, his father, Peter, was ordered to hold him so the beadles could take him to prison in Reigate. Peter was a ferlingsman and also one of the headboroughs. At the same court, John Bruman, Ralph de la Dene, John Geffray, Robert at Hacche, Robert de Rugge and someone surnamed Godwyne came and accepted vacant villein land. All of these

Harrowing and scaring the crows.

---

[33] Poos, Razi & Smith (1996), p.319.

men were specificially named as *nativi comiti*. Subsequent 14[th]C court rolls refer to various people by the name of Brekespere, Pleystowe, Rugge, Sket, Thurbarn and Upbroke as *nativi domini*, so we can assume that, in 1307, Henry Brekespere, Walter Brekespere, Hugh de Pleystowe, Robert at Pleystowe, Robert at Rugge, Roger at Rugge, William le Sket, William Thurbarn and Richard de Upbroke were likewise.

Of course, everyone's social position must have been obvious at the time, especially to the people concerned. Villein status was, after all, one of the flashpoints of the 'Peasants' Revolt' in 1381. However, at this remove, we can only be sure that someone was personally unfree when it is clearly stated.

Family relationships can be equally unclear. Most of the time, it's not obvious from the court rolls how people with the same 'surname' are related. Occasionally, a woman may be referred to as someone's wife or widow; sometimes, a son or daughter may be described as such. The transfer of property, either by deed or through inheritance, can also shed light on the matter. For example, we know that Maurice de Ewekene had at least three children: William, who gave an essoin for his father at the court on 1st March 1282/3, and Maurice and Isabelle, who had inherited his land by 1307. The younger Maurice received the land at Ewekene, while Isabelle had a messuage in the same place. We also know that Gilbert le Spicer had a son called Ralph, to whom he gave a messuage and one acre of land. Very occasionally, links between different families can be surmised. When Henry Oslak gave that acre of land to Emma, daughter of Ralph le Rede, he described it as coming to him by inheritance from Isabelle Crispin of Dorking.[34] An Isabelle Oslak appears (via her attorney) in the 1282-3 court roll, where she was described as the daughter of John Oslak; she brought a plea of debt and another of trespass against Peter le Rede. At the end of July, this debt case was referred to as being between 'Isabelle Pogeys' and 'Peter le Rus'. Is this the same woman? Did Isabelle Oslak marry into the Pogeys family and subsequently into the Crispins?

---

[34] BL 18581.

There were obviously links between the Lovel family and the Strodes. In 1263, Juliana, widow of Walter de la Strode, sued Peter Lovel for one rod of land and a bushel of flour, due as her dower from a mill business. A jury found against her, saying that Peter had tried to give her the flour but she had turned him away. However, she did recover her third share of the mill from Peter by assize of 'novel disseisin' (an action to recover land of which the plaintiff had been recently dispossessed). She received damages of 6s.[35] At the beginning of the 1282-3 manorial year, an enquiry into the extent of Peter Lovel's land was postponed twice. Unfortunately, the details don't survive but it seems that Peter had died before the start of the new court year, leaving his widow and executrix, Alice, and a son, also called Peter. It seems likely that the late Peter was the man who had been sued by Juliana de la Strode twenty years earlier.

In the Extent, Hugh Lovel was described as the son of William at Strode. As we have seen, William was also a miller, running the earl's mills in 1299-1300. So too was Hugh Lovel: he ran the mill at 'Stonlegh' with his business partner, Ralph de Hengham.[36] An oblique reference in the Extent suggests that a Juliana at Strode was Hugh's sister (the Latin is unclear). These details lead to the assumption that there was a second marriage somewhere along the line which linked the two milling families. Hugh had also inherited a tenement from Peter Lovel. Additionally, he held a curtilage in Dorking, while his partner in the mill business, Ralph de Hengham, held property in Dorking and Betchworth.

Meanwhile, in an undated deed, a widow called Beatrix granted half an acre of her land to Walter, miller of Dorking. Beatrix was the daughter of William Sirloc of Dorking and had received the land from Ingerham Lovel 'for her service'. Presumably, she worked for Ingerham; however, that's not all. In another undated deed, Peter de Newdigate claimed the use of a piece of land called 'Hores' in Suthehamsted, through the right of his wife, Emma. Unfortunately for them, it was confirmed by deed that Agnes, grand-daughter of Walter Lovel, was the true heir. Emma's mother had been the

---

[35] SRS XL, pp.27-8 (41).

[36] Stonlegh seems to have been at Pixham. BL 18571 refers to 'the stream that flows to the watermill of Stonerne south of Shiplond'.

aforementioned Beatrix, now described as the 'concubine' of Ingerham Lovel. Emma's claim was, like her, illegitimate.[37] Peter Lovel was a witness to both these deeds. All of which goes to show that medieval relationships could be just as complicated as at any other period.

Protecting goslings from a crow.

---

[37] BL 9003 & 9007. Also see BL 18558.

How to Make a Living

Although the customary tenants carried out most of the farming on the manor, we have little specific information about how they went about it. It must have been a mixture of arable and husbandry, similar to that practised on the earl's demesne land. They would have needed oxen to pull the plough and horses to pull the waggon. We know that Christiana at Wode had sheep because they were reported stolen at the manor court. As well as the non-specific 'beasts' accused of trespassing on people's land, cattle and pigs were paid as heriots. Indeed, there must have been plenty of pigs on the manor because the earl received the substantial sum of £1 6s 7d in pannage for the year 1299-1300. It seems likely that tenants were growing the same mixture of wheat, oats and barley on their land as was grown on the demesne. Barley was the grain most commonly used for brewing; the ale it produced was highly prized and the amount of barley grown in England increased throughout the 14thC.[38] Given the number of residents involved in selling ale (see below), barley must have been widely planted on the manor.

A little more information on farming practice can be deduced from the untangling of Walter Brekespere's inheritance. The contested goods which had belonged to the late William Brekespere were listed in an inventory ordered by the manor court: six horses and one ox (worth 10s), plus one cask, one tub, one pan, one basin, one ploughshare, one cultor and one pruning knife, the total value for the utensils being 9½d. This can't have been everything William owned, especially if he held the Brekespere half-virgate, and a comparison with a previous case may be useful. In 1235, a Dorking man called Peter Snoke, who also held half a virgate of land, was found guilty of larceny and had to leave the country. His chattels were confiscated: four cows, two oxen, two draught animals, thirteen ewes and five marks-worth of grain. All these chattels were valued at 100s.[39]

Although the business of the manor was primarily agricultural, there were other ways to earn a living. Brewing ale provided year-round opportunities to make money: the process takes several days and the

---

[38] Campbell (2000), pp.223 & 244.
[39] SRS XXXII, p.411.

product doesn't keep, so there was a steady market. Even those who regularly brewed their own would need to supplement their stocks at different times.[40]   Legislation known as the Assize of Bread and Ale was introduced in the 13thC to regulate the trade. Quantity and quality were to be measured and prices fixed, depending on the price of grain. In rural areas, the assize was enforced through the manor court and quickly developed into a licensing system. All those who brewed ale for sale had to call the aletaster to test each batch and to check that they were selling by correct measures. The assize also regulated the weight and price of bread.

In Dorking, the aletasters were elected each year. The 1282-3 court roll doesn't name them but in later years there were two for the town and two for Waldeborough. Only eleven of the seventeen court sessions include aletasters' reports and only one included brewers from the Walde. This may explain why some of the fees in 1282-3 were rather steep. 2d or 3d was the norm but some were set at 6d; perhaps these were carried over. Sometimes, the fees were waived, with the aleseller being listed as 'pauper' (too poor to pay the fine). The process was obviously supervised by the steward: at the end of July, the list of brewers was held over until the next court because he wasn't in attendance.

A total of sixty-nine brewers were named in the 1282-3 court roll. Thirteen of them were women: as it was based on household activity, women were often involved in aleselling. Three of the women were widows, all called Agnes: widow Chapman, the widow of John Osbern and the widow of John Quarreor. Forty-six individuals were named only once, suggesting that they were selling the surplus from their own household production. Those most often featured were Peter Mentenaunt and Peter Tanner, who both appear five times, and Gilbert Crul (jnr and snr), Adam le Frend, Robert Nower, Mabil Osbern and Elias le Seler, all of whom were named four times during the course of the year. Certain families are well-represented in the lists. Alongside the aforementioned Cruls, Alice at Flusshe was named with Ralph and William de la Flusshe. Thomas and Mabil Osbern were both named, as were Peter and Richard Bruggesulle,

---

[40] Bennett (1986), p.21.

Richard and Robert le Clerc and John, Peter and William Tanner. Nicholas le Chapman, who was presumably related by marriage to the widow Chapman, was twice required to answer the charge that he had weighed bread without a warrant. ('Chapman' means someone who sells but this looks like a surname.)

There is little direct information in the court roll about other trades being carried out in Dorking. Two attorneys called Geoffrey de Middleton and James at Boxe appeared at the court on behalf of several clients. William Berfot was named as a tanner when his opponent in a court case was essoined. Other than that, the only clues we have are found in people's names. A number of men seem to be identified by their occupations, such as Robert le Boucher, Simon le Carpenter or Peter le Carter. However, there was also a William le Carter; was he in the trade or was 'Carter' his and Peter's surname? Were the four men surnamed 'Sutor' all working as shoemakers or was it their family name? Presumably, Robert Faber was the smith, Gilbert Peletor the skinner and John and William le Pistur were bakers but we can't be sure. Other names which could signify an occupation but might simply be surnames include Peter Isemonger (ironmonger), William Fletcher (arrowmaker) and Juliana Cultrix (nurse or fosterer).

An inquiry into stallage at the View of Frankpledge revealed that at least ten of the brewers were selling in the marketplace: Walter Alard, Richard de Brugesulle, Agnes, widow Chapman, Richard Gamelys, William de Molend', John Moris, Robert Nower, Emma, daughter of Rose, Elias le Seler and William Tanner. *Molendinum* is medieval Latin for 'mill', so this may refer to William at Strode. Dorking held its twice-weekly market in Suthestret and the town had no borough charter, so the market was run directly as part of the manor. In 1282, it was 'farmed' to Adam de la Sonde and Peter de Hambreche; they paid 20 marks per year for three years, starting at Michaelmas. As well as the aforementioned ten brewers, Agnes de la Lofte paid 2s to William Crispin for a market stall. We don't know what she was selling.

There were also shops in the town. The Extent lists at least ten among the freehold properties, where they are always referred to as 'shopa'. The word was originally Old English (*sheopa*) when it meant a booth. Medieval shops consisted of a board which could be let down on market days, allowing the shopkeeper to serve the customer without the latter actually coming in to the premises. There also seems to have been a 'seld', a stone building set at right angles to the street in which a number of stalls were available, rather like a bazaar or souk; we know this because the manorial accounts of 1262-3 refer to repairs to a lock or bolt for the 'seld in the marketplace'.[41] The market-house was known as the Tolhous. Although a later version was purpose-built in the middle of the high street, the medieval one was probably converted from an ordinary house.[42]

A shoemaker's shop. The original illustration is post-medieval but shows how medieval shops functioned.

---

[41] There is another reference to a 'seld with appurtenences' in the Surrey Eyre for the same year but this may refer to a shop rather than a larger building. It was the subject of an inheritance dispute and rented out to a William at Frithe. (The 1263 Surrey Eyre, p.42.)

[42] The later market-house was demolished in 1813 but has been identified from paintings as probably dating to the 16thC. It was positioned in East Street. There is some question about where the medieval market was held but the shape of South Street supports the idea of the market site being there.

The Church

On Shrove Tuesday, a football match took place in Dorking. A rowdy and bruising affair, it pitched players from one half of the town against the other, ranging up and down the high street or perhaps taking place in nearby fields. Such games used to be common throughout the country and, unlike many 'ancient' customs that turn out to be much more recent in origin, Shrove Tuesday football is well-attested in the medieval period.[43] Shrove Tuesday was also the day for eating up foods prohibited during the Lenten fast and for being shriven (making confession and receiving absolution) in preparation for taking communion on Easter Day.

The church year started, as it still does, at Advent. This was a period of penitence leading up to the celebrations of Christmas and Epiphany. In February, parishioners brought candles to church to celebrate Candlemas. Lent was a period of fasting and reflection, beginning on Ash Wednesday. After Palm Sunday, the solemnity of Good Friday was followed by the joy of the resurrection at Easter. Attendance at Christmas, Easter, Whitsun and the parish church's dedicatory feast was compulsory for the laity.

Dorking parish church was built of local flint on a cruciform pattern, with a tower at the meeting point of chancel, nave and north and south transepts. The building would have been open every day, morning and afternoon, as the clergy were expected to perform the Office each day: matins first thing and evensong at three or four in the afternoon. Daily mass wasn't obligatory but it was popular with the laity, despite not being very participatory for the congregation. If it were held in Dorking during the week, it would have been a low mass (said, not sung). Mass on Sunday was a much more elaborate affair, sung in plainsong chant throughout. Parishioners were welcome to attend any service but were expected to go to Sunday mass; frequent absences would be reported to the church authorities, unless you were a shepherd who found regular attendance impossible. Even if you weren't particularly devout, there were reasons to go: announcements from the pulpit included upcoming holy days, the next manor court and occasional royal proclamations.

---

[43] The earliest reference is in London c.1180 (Roud (2006), pp.53-5). The earliest reference to the Dorking game dates to the 19thC.

Unfortunately, all our information about medieval worship comes from cathedrals and urban parishes. In an agricultural parish, it's reasonable to assume the parishioners lit candles in the church on Plough Sunday (the start of the agricultural year) and dragged the plough round the church on Plough Monday. On Palm Sunday, willow branches would have been collected for a procession around the churchyard. Even wider-ranging was the Rogationtide procession which started at the church and made its way around the parish. In Dorking, it probably progressed to the chapel at Ewekene, via a series of way-stations.

When Dorking manor was given to the de Warennes by King William Rufus, patronage of the church came too. Isabelle, widow of the second earl, then granted the church to the Priory of St Pancras in Lewes. This house of Cluniac monks had been founded by the first earl and countess and Dorking church was one of many valuable gifts made by the de Warennes to their new foundation. The parish of Dorking lay in the Winchester diocese and, in the 1190s, the gift of Dorking church was confirmed by bishop Godfrey, with Lewes Priory's rights being converted into a £6 annual pension. In 1291, the church and the chapel at Ewekene were valued at the large sum of £66 13s 4d (only Chertsey and Farnham came close in the Guildford deanery, while Leatherhead was rated at £34 13s 4d).[44] The chapel at Ewekene was built in the 12thC, probably by Lewes Priory, to make churchgoing easier for those who lived south of the Homwode. Chapels were subordinate to the parish church: the chaplain could not conduct baptisms, marriages or burials and had to pay a sum to the rector. The earliest chaplain for whom we have any information was called Henry. (He was the chaplain named in the court roll as an alleged executor of William de Brugesulle's will.) 'Ewekene' and 'Capel' were already interchangeable: Henry is referred to by both names.

Dorking parish had both a rector and a vicar, the rector being presented by Lewes Priory. The position was obviously worth having, as a document from the 1260s records that Richard de Honeton was granted the Dorking benefice at the request of the Pope and held it 'for some time' before giving

---

[44] Taxatio Ecclesiastica 1291.

it up to another Richard, papal subdeacon and notary (and nephew of an Italian cardinal).[45] By 1280, part of the rectorship, worth 20 marks, was held by Bogo de Clare.[46] He was a member of the Anglo-Norman aristocracy, notorious for holding multiple livings despite never having been ordained. His household accounts for 1284-6 reveal that Henry the chaplain paid him 13s 4d for the position at Ewekene; whether this was a one-off or an annual payment isn't clear.[47] Then, in the 1290s, John de Warenne became rector. He was an illegitimate son of the earl who was ordained underage, held a number of benefices and was frequently in debt.[48]

The role of rector was a post-Conquest innovation. He was not required to be resident in the parish and, in the early 12[th]C, the custom of appointing a vicar to do the actual work became widespread. Unfortunately, we have no information on any early vicars of Dorking (unless we count the priest called William who witnessed two grants during the first half of the 12thC).[49] Funds were raised primarily through the collection of tithes, although there were other sources of income, such as the collection of the second best beast when a tenant died or offerings made at certain services. Tithes were divided between the rector and the vicar. The rector got the 'great tithes': grain. The vicar got the 'lesser tithes', including young animals, wool, dairy products and eggs. The church's glebe land lay to the west of the town and would have been the site of the tithe barn and, presumably, the vicar's accommodation.

---

[45] Papal Register 29, vol I, pp.404-418.
[46] Rolls and register of Bishop Oliver Sutton, p.3.
[47] Giuseppi (1920), p.34.
[48] Papal Registers, vol I, p.417.
[49] Blair (1980), p.116.

The Wider World

The lord of the manor throughout these years was John de Warenne, Earl of Surrey, who had inherited the title from his father in 1240. Married to the half-sister of Henry III, he was generally in favour with the crown and, in 1275, entertained Edward I at Reigate castle. As father-in-law to John Balliol, the earl was particularly active in Scotland, where he and the king supported Balliol's claim to the throne. The earl was sent north to recover Dunbar Castle in 1296 and, after the king went to France, was appointed governor of Scotland. The following year, he sent an army to fight William Wallace and subsequently joined Edward I to lead the English troops to victory at Falkirk. The earl was predeceased by his wife and son so, when he died in 1304, the title passed to his grandson, also called John.

The earl initially had his London house in Tooley Street, close to that of the Prior of Lewes.[50] By 1274, this property belonged to a John de Boklaunde; the earl obtained the Manor of Kennington in 1276, so perhaps he then used that manor as his 'London' residence.[51] It was there he died, after which the manor was given to Edward II. The Dorking accounts of 1299-1300 include a reference to John le Nywater, reeve of Kennington, and to substantial loads of talwode being sent there 'for the use of the lord earl'. As we have seen, firewood was regularly carried from Dorking to Kingston for further transport downriver: the journey took a day, through Leatherhead and Chessington. The parish church at Kingston received many gifts from successful merchants, including one Baldwin 'Buscarius' (woodmonger), citizen of London, whose deed was witnessed by Ralph de Dorking and John le Tymbermonger.[52]

A number of merchants who had their origins in Dorking appear in the London records. Several of them were woolmongers. Odo de Dorking was a citizen and merchant of London active in the 1270s, who was involved in bringing in a clerk called John de Bletchingley to answer to the authorities regarding an accidental death.[53] Another woolmonger was John de

---

[50] Schofield (2003), p.231.
[51] Pedes Finium, p.51 (34) & CCR Ed II, vol II, p.347 (380).
[52] Heales (1883), p.47.
[53] Letter Book B, p.257.

Dorking, who appears in the records between the 1270s and early 1300s, where he was described as both a merchant of Dorking and a citizen and merchant of London. He had permission to export wool abroad and was one of four men involved in a dispute with the Duke of Brabant over wool worth £177 6s 3d which had been seized unlawfully. [54] He was owed money for a doublet and gambeson, so perhaps he was also a mercer. [55] John held land near the Greyfriars; whether he or Odo still lived in or held property on Dorking manor is impossible to say.[56] Another woolmonger named John at Dene de Dorking leased a tenement in Seething Lane for sixteen years.[57] He might be the John at Dene who appeared in the 1282-3 court roll giving an essoin for Peter le Rede in his plea of debt against Isabelle Oslak and another for William at Boxe in his case against John Emme. William at Boxe and John at Dene were also among several men accused of hunting and selling the earl's rabbits in 1282.

London in the 1550s, showing St Paul's and part of the Vintry.

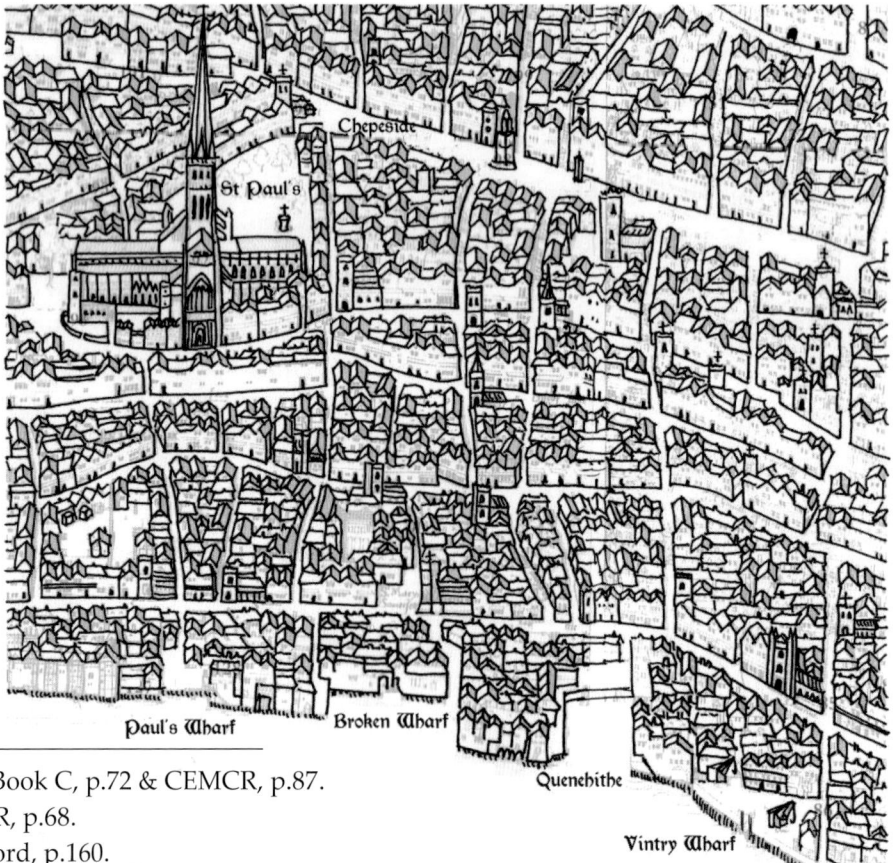

[54] Letter Book C, p.72 & CEMCR, p.87.
[55] CEMCR, p.68.
[56] Kingsford, p.160.
[57] Letter Book A, p.150.

Before the Black Death: 1308-1349

At Michaelmas in the year 1330, Walter at Hulle, reeve of Dorking, presented his annual account. His tenancy lay south of the Homwode, next to that of William Thurbarn, who served as beadle of Walde that year. The beadle of Dorking was William le Fust, who may have lived in Holowestret, and they were all overseen by the earl's steward, whose name was Henry. The account prepared by Walter was laid out in a way that had obviously become the norm and would continue to be so throughout our period and beyond. (Evidently, there were pattern books available for clerks to follow, for accounts and for court rolls.) Whether Walter drew up the account himself or kept tallies and then had a clerk write it all down is not known. Either way, Henry the steward would have kept a close eye on him, performing an audit part way through the year.

On the surface, things didn't look too good. Receipts totalled £98 16s 7¾d, while expenses were £95 12s 4d. Only £3 was carried over from the previous year, showing that the downturn wasn't sudden. Receipts were rather small because prices for grain were low and Walter didn't record any sales of timber or charcoal. On the other hand, expenses were also low and would have been much lower had they not included payments for a debt. The earl owed money to a knight called Sir John de Wysham and some of the payments to repay the debt were being taken from Dorking manorial receipts. In 1329-30, the sum was £56 12s 2½d.

The debt dated back several years. In 1311, a charter was confirmed which listed fifty-one Dorking tenants from whose rent £20 was to be granted for life to Sir John.[58] Including both freehold and customary tenants, this provides a useful comparison with the information in the Extent, not least because the amounts taken from each tenant vary, giving some idea of what levels of rent they were paying.[59] According to Walter's accounts, there was also another arrangement to grant Sir John 100 marks from the rents of tenants in Dorking, Betchworth and Reigate. Sir John de Wysham was a knight who held various pieces of land from the earl,

---

[58] CPR Ed II, vol I, p.405.
[59] See Appendix A.

including the manor of Wikham in Sussex, 400 acres at Holt, near Wrexham in North Wales, and another 400 acres near Castle Lyon in Ireland. He died in 1334.

Walter's job wasn't easy. The climate had become more unpredictable compared with the previous century, with wetter and cooler summers shortening the growing season. Livestock was affected by disease, although it seems that herds were quickly restocked after the famine years of 1315-22. Certainly, levels of stock in the store in 1330 are comparable with previous years. However, Walter had to buy in wheat and oat seed, as well as maslin (a mixture of rye and wheat) and sixteen cartloads of straw to sustain the oxen, cows and bullocks 'by default of forage in the store'. This situation may partly have arisen because most of the hay in the Burnemed had been suddenly carried away by a flood. At least prices were low, although that also meant that Walter didn't get much for the grain he sold: 2½d per quarter for wheat, 1½d for barley, 2d for vetch and 1d for oats. The hides of an ox and a calf also had to be sold; they had died of murrain, the endemic disease affecting cattle and sheep which rendered the meat worthless. However, dairy receipts were good: £6 12s 6d was raised from a herd of 29 cows.

Stacking grain at harvest.

At the Manor Court

Unfortunately, very few court records have survived between 1283 and 1365 and those only partially: there are four reports from 1342 and three from 1344-5, stitched together in the same roll. All are damaged and difficult to decipher. They are also less detailed that those from 1282-3, which isn't unexpected as court rolls gradually became more formulaic and repetitive during the 14thC. Interestingly, the dates of the 1342 courts are expressed with reference to church feast days (Holy Trinity, St Barnabas, the Translation of Thomas the Martyr and Lammasday), while those from 1344-5 refer to the numerical date (13th December, 3rd January and 24th January). Either there was a new clerk in Dorking or the old one decided to change to the numerical system somewhere between 1342 and 1344.

The court was still being held every three weeks and the cases dealt with were similar to those found in the previous roll. However, the number of essoins presented for absence from the court was significantly higher than in 1282-3. Also, for the first time, we have references to people paying for 'commutation of suit of court': permission to stay away from the manor court for the rest of the year. Two tenants (names unclear) paid 2d in December 1344 and Alice Breggesulle gave 3d in the following January for the same. It seems likely that the reeve was now presiding over the court; there is one reference to the steward, when a day was appointed for him to make a judgement on some bread.

Tenants cutting timber without permission continued to be a problem for the earl. In 1342, John Baroun and William Doulyng were each fined 6d for cutting two faggots of wood in the Homwode, while Walter at Hulle and Adam le Stub were fined 3d and 4d respectively for felling an oak and a beech without permission. In 1344, Robert Brouman and Robert at Bere each paid 4d for cutting down an oak. No cases of poaching appear in these limited court rolls but it seems unlikely that the problem had ceased. In 1324, two Dorking men named as Robert Coumber and Simon le Souter were accused by William le Latymer, lord of Wotton, of poaching on his land.[60]

---

[60] CPR EdII, vol IV, p.448.

Twelve pleas of trespass were in progress in these partial rolls. William de Brugges brought two cases, one against Richard le Baker and the other against Alice Hurlewyne. In both, he alleged that each of them had intruded on his land with a member of their households and hoed his rye, trampling it underfoot and causing losses worth 6d and 12d respectively. Both of the accused denied it and brought pledges in support. Richard le Baker was subsequently fined for not pleading his case in court; Alice Hurlewyne was aquitted of the charge.

In 1342, Roger Jerconville (spelled Gerpennylle) brought cases against John Heggere and Richard le Muleward. Muleward was distrained of a bronze pot and Heggere was summoned to court but neither attended. (We don't know the outcome in either case.) In 1344, John Deth was accused of trespass by John Bonet and by Alice Gauge. Bonets and Gauges are both on the southern edge of the manor; perhaps John Deth held one of the properties later known as 'Ridge' or 'Fylls'. A levy on his goods and chattels was made in the first case but Alice Gauge settled out of court. Meanwhile, William Bronnot asked for the rolls to be examined, so he could prove that John at Dene had removed hay from his land three years previously to his loss of 12d.

Even with a mere handful of court records surviving from the 1340s, it is clear that the manor court was being used more frequently for private pleas of debt. Three courts in 1342 include details of thirteen cases. Roger Taillour brought six of them, five in his name; in the sixth he acted as attorney for Thomas de Wonham. Slightly strangely, Thomas attended court himself, admitted the debt and settled it. Thomas wasn't the only plaintiff from outside the manor: William de Grenestede brought two separate cases against Simon Smyth and Richard Smyth, while Henry Glover of Leatherhead did likewise against John Bishop of Ashtead. Why the latter two men should be embroiled in a debt case in Dorking is unclear, although Henry Glover's pledges were local (William Bacheler and John Coillard) and his attorney was William Chert. Conversely, the seven cases described in the three 1344-5 courts mostly involve people from the manor: John Belde versus Roger Whytyng, Adam Carpenter versus Stephen at Nouere, Maurice Compeden versus Thomas at Conygrove and Peter Kene,

John Gilbert versus Thomas at Flusshe, Edward at Sonde versus William de Brugge and Robert Weston versus Laurence Lynne.

No View of Frankpledge survives from these years, so we don't know if any violence took place. However, the accounts of 1329-30 include the cost of a new 'trebuchetto', made by order of Henry the steward and paid by indenture of Robert de Weston, the constable of Reigate castle. This was a 'cucking-stool': a wooden seat onto which malefactors were tied and paraded humiliatingly around the town. The cucking-stool tended to be used to punish women, especially for being a common scold. Although men could also be punished in this way, they were more likely to be put into the stocks or pillory.[61]

Some common scolds gossipping.

---

[61] The earliest reference to stocks in Dorking of which the author is aware is found in the 1255 Surrey Eyre (JUST 1/872), when a man caught for theft was placed in them. (With thanks to Giles Graham-Brown for this information.) It has been suggested the stocks might have been placed outside the cotland later known as the Stockhouse. The Dorking accounts of 1391-2 refer to ironwork being bought for them.

The Demesne

One of the most obvious differences between the previous set of accounts and those of 1329-30 is that the hens, capons, eggs, gilded spurs, cumin and talsides of firewood which had been physically gathered in the store were now represented by monetary sums (which explains how a tenant might owe half an egg). Instead of 96 hens, the earl received 16s. Instead of six capons, he got 18d; instead of 422 eggs, 21d. The gilded spurs were replaced by 12d and the cumin by a penny. (The pepper isn't mentioned, although it reappears in later sets of accounts, rated at 2s per lb.) These amounts had been set out in the Extent; indeed, it seems likely that part of the purpose of that document was to specify the new cash-based regime.

Something similar was going on with the agricultural labour owed by the customary tenants and cottars. Their work had been described and valued in the Extent, the total worth being £6 7s 9d. Some commutation of labour was recorded in the 1299-1300 accounts but, by 1329-30, the system was obviously fully in place. A total of £6 1s 3½d was recorded as received from the tenants instead of various forms of labour services. However, this didn't mean that the tenants were free from their obligations. The accounts also show a series of payments to them to do the work; for example, 10s 10½d was received in lieu of muck-spreading and then 7s was paid to thirty-two of the tenants to carry out the job. In that case, the earl got the better of the deal; in others, the sums were the same, as when eight acres of hay were mown and gathered and 11d was both received and paid for the work.

Mowing the meadow.

It may seem overly complicated for these payments to be recorded as receipts and then again as expenses but it meant the earl retained his right to his tenants' labour and, presumably, that those who could afford it could turn work down. In 1329-30, the earl paid out £1 and 1¾d to tenants for work, some of it as piece-work, so he definitely came out ahead. Whether these sums were actually paid in and out or just tallied in the paperwork is hard to tell. If the former, then the reeve may have ended up out of pocket on some transactions, as when 2s 6d was recorded as paid to tenants for ploughing but was then cancelled because the work had actually been done by the earl's ploughteam.

As in 1299-1300, the ploughman was paid 5s per year and the man driving the plough 6d, plus 4s 4d for drink-money. The earl also employed a shepherd at 4s 6d per year and a swineherd at 2s per year. These employees also received a dole of grain for pottage. The ploughmen and harrower received about a quarter of grain per week; the ploughteam for ten weeks, the harrower for one. The shepherd, dairyman and swineherd received less: the shepherd got about 2½ bushels per week over twelve weeks, whereas the dairyman and swineherd were obviously employed all year round. They received a total of 4 quarters 6 bushels and 3 quarters 2 bushels respectively.

Apart from the money paid to Sir John de Wysham and the abovementioned wages, there were other expenses. Some were plough expenses: one plough had to be mended, involving buying a new wheel, and another plough had to be made new. Horseshoes were bought for a stot and a mare, plus shoes for two oxen. 4s 10½d was spent on two pairs of new wheels, iron cleats and axle grease for the cart. The manorial buildings also required extensive repairs. Walter Squier and his son were paid 5s 4d to reinforce the structure supporting a solar (upper room) at the 'manor house' by inserting three new posts. (This building is usually assumed to be the steward's chamber.) They also had to make supporting beams for the ox-shed and dairy, after which Nicholas de Eggesworthe was paid 21d to whitewash the new structure.

Of course, repairing the ox-shed and the barn was another task allotted to the customary tenants: 2s 5½d was recorded as both received and paid out for their work. Repairs were also necessary at both mills. The Medmell needed a new roof; it was obviously thatched, as withies were gathered by the roofer and two cartloads of straw bought for the purpose. A water post was made by the carpenter, by order of Henry the steward and Robert the constable. Substantial land-works were also carried out: the embankment was dammed and the ground dug and carried away. At the Estmell, the waterwheel and the cogwheel had to be mended, using sawn planks and nails. Mill repairs totalled £4 7s 4d; this was expensive, although less so than in 1299-1300.

95 acres of land were under the plough during this year. Apart from the Parrok, all the fields listed as suitable for arable in the Extent were planted, resulting in 11 acres of barley, 26 acres of wheat, 5½ acres of vetch and 52½ acres of oats. The amount of meadow was almost the same as set out in the Extent: ten acres in 1329-30 compared with twelve acres in 1307. However, a great deal more land was laid down to pasture. There were by now at least 120 sheep on the demesne, guarded by the shepherd when they were out in the earl's pasture. The store account also refers to horses, cattle and swine: a stot, seven mares and a colt; fourteen oxen, a bull, 29 cows, five bullocks and five calves; and thirteen swine and 27 piglets.

There were also hares, rabbits, pheasants and partridges in the earl's warren: he complained several times in 1324 and 1325 about poaching by various unnamed persons.[62] Catching the malefactors was the responsibility of Richard Godwyne, the assistant warrener. He would have lived in the lodge, which was positioned on a slope on the edge of the demesne land and overlooking the warren. The building had to be repaired in 1329-30, at a cost of 13s 3d, with nails, boards and chalk all being bought for the work by order of Robert the constable and indentured by Walter the reeve. The hedges around the warren were also lopped and pleached, at a cost of 12s. Unfortunately, the earl's rabbits don't seem to have made him any money that year as no sales were recorded.

---

[62] CPR Ed II, vol IV, p.448 & vol V, pp.223 & 293.

Who Lived on the Manor?

In 1332, a lay subsidy was raised. This was a tax whereby a percentage of the value of a householder's moveable goods was levied: a tenth if you lived in a large town, a fifteenth in the country. In this case, the money was needed to fund the war in Scotland. The resulting lists of heads of household are renowned among medievalists as being particularly accurate and therefore useful. The Dorking section names 96 taxpayers, ranging from Robert at Sonde (who paid 8s 3½d) to Peter and Ralph Spicer (who both paid 8d).[63] Only those whose personal goods were worth more than 10s were taxed, so less affluent households did not pay the subsidy. Despite this, it allows us for the first time to get a clear impression of how many people lived on the manor.

Of those 96 taxpayers, 28 appear to be holders of customary tenancies, which leaves 68 freeholders. If we assume that most, if not all, of the freeholders living in Dorking had sufficient moveable goods to be taxed, that would mean these 68 individuals comprise most or all of the freeholders living on the manor. Given that the earl received £36 12s 6½d in rent and 4s 6d Romescot in 1329-30, we can also assume that the 38 customary tenancies and 17 cotlands were all occupied. Added together, this gives us a total of 123 heads of household. It's usual to multiply such a figure by five to reach an estimate of total population, which suggests 615 people were living on the Dorking manor around the year 1330. This is a reasonable number, given the size of the manor, but it's bound to be an underestimate: it doesn't include servants, those of moderate means renting property in the private sector or the very poor (apart from the cottars).

An increase in population since the 1280s is suggested by the fact that the three original boroughs of East, Chipping and Walde had been joined by a fourth, called 'Foreign'. We know this because among the alesellers listed in 1342 was one 'William Fissehar de Forine', so named to distinguish him from another 'William le Fisher'. Covering an area just south of the town, Foreignborough had been renamed 'Homewood borough' by the 16thC.

---

[63] SRS XI, pp.31-2. See Appendix B.

According to the 1329-30 accounts, the rent due for both pieces of land held by knight's fee had been paid. Robert Bonet also paid the 1332 subsidy but no-one surnamed 'at Chert' is listed, unless the 'Henry at Clause?' in the printed version is actually a misreading of Henry at Chert. (This is much more likely than it might seem.) Many of the freeholders named in the subsidy are familiar: John Chapman, Thomas at Churchgate, Maurice de Ewekene, Alice Hurlewyne, Juliana Mum, various Sondes and John Stub all appear. Hugh Lovel is named as 'Hugh at Strode'.

As for the customary tenants, the lay subsidy reveals four potential candidates for the three virgaters: Hugh at Pleystowe, Henry de Langshete, Roger de Langshete and Stephen de Wadelshurst. Sixteen of the surnames associated with the half-virgates and furlongs are present but fifteen are not; as all bar one (Stel) continue to appear in manorial records, this presumably means they didn't meet the 10s threshold. The 'missing' names include Walter at Hulle, the reeve in 1329-30, Richard Godwyne, assistant warrener, and William Thurbarn, beadle of Walde. William le Fust, beadle of Dorking, did contribute to the subsidy; he must have held a customary tenancy in order to be elected to serve as beadle but was obviously more well-to-do than his fellow officials. Avelina at Hethe did not pay the subsidy, despite the fact that she made a will in 1344 and her executors owed heriot. Her will doesn't survive; perhaps she came into an inheritance after 1332.

Of course, it cannot be assumed that everyone known by a particular surname was still living on the plot designated in the Extent. Henry and Peter Godard, who were presumably related to the Peter Godard who held a furlong in 1307, had exchanged some land with Henry at Dene seven or eight years before 1342; we have no further details, apart from the fact that previous court rolls were being examined to assess the facts in the case. The Godards weren't the only customary tenants doing land deals (with the earl's permission, of course). Henry Langshete leased three fields to Roger Roulf for thirty years; he received a fixed payment and Roger paid 6s 8d (half a mark) to the earl. Roger was also assured access with a waggon to the land. Richard Brekespere leased five acres of land from Robert at Chert. Called 'Westlond', it lay next to Richard's tenement; he had to pay rent to the earl and both Richard and Robert paid the entry fine of 3s 4d. Freeholders were also extending their properties. John Stub received a messuage and part of a croft called 'Westfelde' from William le Isemonger, the messuage being next to his tenement at the Homwode.[64] In 1326, Hugh de Netelfold granted to John at Homwode a field that lay between his land, the earl's, the woods and 'a certain road which leads to the house of William de Bruggesulle, next to the house of William Brekespere'.[65] As previously mentioned, land in Stoneylond could be leased. Isabelle, widow of William Clerk, surrendered half an acre for the use of William Janeway, while Henry Bynorthebroke leased another half an acre to John Chapman. John and his heirs were to hold it in villeinage for fifteen years, for which he paid a 6d entry fine. There was also an enquiry into 22 acres held by Matilda Churchgate, with two references to the rolls being examined.

In 1344, the earl alienated the Grenehurst tenement, which means that somebody bought it outright (like Henry de Sutbury fifty years before). We don't know who the new owner was or how much he or she paid to be released from all the customary dues and services associated with the property but, in 1390, it was sold on for 100 marks in silver. There was also a quitrent of 5d per year plus a red rose at midsummer (which was still being referred to in the 18thC).[66]

The freehold property market continued to thrive. In particular, the Sonde family amassed more rents and property, especially in the area of Dorking known as 'Hamstede' or 'Suthehamsted'.[67] They weren't the only people with interests in that part of town. In 1323, Gilbert Doulyng granted Robert Hurlewyne and his wife, Alice, a curtilage in Suthamstede, next to one which had been granted to the couple by Robert's father twenty years earlier.[68] He was also called Robert and held a number of pieces of land, including those next to the curtilage he gave his son and daughter-in-law.

---

[64] BL 18614, 18616. See also BL 9037.

[65] Bray notebook.

[66] PRO CP 25/1/231 & SRO 196/3/1.

[67] BL 18597, 18622, 18629 and 18630. See also BL 9011, 9012, 9019 and 18603. BL 18563 refers to the hide of land called Hamsted, then held by Robert de la Sonde, chaplain, from the Prior and Convent of Holy Trinity, London.

[68] BL 18613 and 9017.

Robert, snr also had a house and a tenement in Suthestret; he gave another son, William, the right to rent a house in between the two. However, he didn't 'own' that property: it belonged to Henry Whytyng, who received 6d per annum, which he subsequently granted to the Sondes.[69] It was Alice Hurlewyne who paid the lay subsidy, so it seems that Robert, jnr had died before 1332; she also appeared as an aleseller in the 1342 court roll (as had her father-in-law in 1282-3). There was another branch of the Hurlewyne family on the manor: Gilbert Hurlewyne and his wife, Matilda, held half an acre of land in 1307 and their daughter, Agnes, held a curtilage.

We are usually unable to pinpoint the position of freehold properties in the town but there is an exception. In 1649, a plot on West Street was named as 'Godfreys'. This seems to be the messuage and curtilage granted by John Chapman, snr to Walter Godefray in March 1351. John had inherited it from his father, Peter Chapman, and it lay between the Sonde family land to the south and the tenement held by Thomas le Fust to the west.[70]

Freehold property continued to be held as an investment by people who didn't live on the manor. A Thomas le Nolde of Cranleigh received a piece of land at Ewekene called the 'Southagh' from Richard at Homwode in 1346. The transaction was carried out by his attorney, William Paon, clerk of Dorking.[71] William would have had to come to the manor court to show the deed and swear fealty to the earl; in 1342, William at Nore, parson of Bisley church, was requested to attend court, in order to show how he had acquired 48 acres of land from Thomas de Compedon's man. His attorney came but didn't bring the deed, so William at Nore continued to be summoned to the court. Women were also involved in such transactions, as when Albreda de Durfolde leased an acre of land to John Chapman, jnr for seven years or when Isabelle Skynnere leased half an acre of pasture to Richard at Sonde for two years. Both transactions required the earl's permission.

---

[69] BL 9018.

[70] BL 9038. Perhaps the latter was the customary tenancy previously held by William le Fust, beadle?

[71] Bray notebook. Some details are indestinct, particularly surnames.

As we've seen with the Hurlewynes, land could be granted to a son or daughter, perhaps to set them up in life. Thus, in June 1344, Stephen Peter gave a messuage to his son, Walter. The following February, Gilbert le Tannere did the same, granted a messuage and curtilage to his daughter, Isabelle.[72]

Chasing a fox stealing a duck.

---

[72] Recorded in the 16thC notes on the court rolls.

How to Make a Living

In April 1318, Gunnild at Dene made her last testament.[73] It wasn't a will because she had no landed property to convey; all her bequests were either in cattle or coin. She left her soul to Almighty God and asked for her body to be buried in the graveyard of Newdigate church, from which we can deduce that she must have lived on the eastern edge of the manor or perhaps came originally from Newdigate. She left 6d to the parish chapel (probably the one at Ewekene), as well as 15d ploughscot and 8s to pay for candles to be lit before the altar, without specifying at which church.[74] Her charitable bequests consisted of £1 6s 8d to be distributed to the poor a week after her burial and 10s the following year. She also left 6s 6d to thirteen poor laymen of the parish, which might be a reference to the thirteen cottars who occur time after time in the Dorking manorial accounts in receipt of a meal at Christmas.

Gunnild also made a series of personal bequests. Gilbert, Nicholas and Robert at Dene each received a cow and a calf. William de Newdigate received a cow and a two year old bullock. Gunnild's daughter, Mabel, received 'my whole share of four cows', while Simon, son of John Rolf, Robert, son of William de Newdigate, and Matilda, daughter of Richard le Yonge, each received a half share of eight calves for eight years. Finally, Rose at Hulle and Richard de Newdigate were given 12d each and John le Rolf received 6d, with the residue of Gunnild's estate left to be used by her executors for the good of her soul. The executors were William de Newdigate and John Rolf.

How should we interpret this document? 'At Dene' (here spelled 'atte Denne') was a common surname in Dorking and other nearby manors. Gunnild doesn't identify herself as daughter, wife or widow in the preamble to the testament; however, the church supported the right of wives to make wills or testaments separately from their husbands, so that might not be significant.[75] Presumably, the whole or half shares in cattle refer to dairy profits rather than anything more macabre. Did Gunnild

---

[73] BL Add Ch 17295.

[74] Ploughscot was payable fifteen days after Easter.

[75] Barron (2017), p.370.

inherit an interest in a herd, along with her male relatives? Were Gilbert, Nicholas and Robert her brothers? If so, they were not named as such in her testament. The Rolfs and de Newdigates crop up occasionally in the Dorking manorial rolls; the at Hulles and le Yonges more frequently. Did Gunnild leave half shares to Simon, Robert and Matilda in order to give them a start in life? Finally, can we say anything about Gunnild's social status? She bequeathed a total of £2 15s 5d: £2 3s 2d to the poor, 9s 9d to the church and 2s 6d to individuals. This was a not inconsiderable sum but further than that we cannot go.

The Denes feature throughout the Dorking manorial records but it's not clear how they were connected to Gunnild or the others mentioned in her testament. In the Extent, Peter at Dene is described as holding a furlong of land while Odo and Thomas each held a cotland. (Thomas seems to have inherited his cotland from Geoffrey and Guthra, while Odo was the son of Peter who refused to take a piece of land and was wanted by the beadle.) Peter appears throughout the 1282-3 court roll; so too does John at Dene, who, with his son, Adam, was one of the witnesses who failed to support Peter le Rede in court. There was also the William de la Dene who was wodeward in 1299-1300.

Another branch of the Denes is revealed in an undated deed of c.1280, when Agnes, daughter of Richard de la Dene, gave a croft in Suthehamsted to a Robert de Guldeford and his wife, Matilda. They paid half a mark but also had to give 3d per annum to the earl and a gillyflower (carnation) to Agnes and her heirs on the Feast of John the Baptist (24th June or midsummer). Agnes sealed the document and it was witnessed by various well-to-do men, including two of the Sondes and Nicholas de Westone.[76] By the 1330s and 40s, another Peter at Dene was active. He paid 8d in the lay subsidy of 1332 and was busy expanding his holding, receiving several acres from Nicholas le Noble and a John Payne. Both he and John at Dene appear in the 1342 court roll.

Due to the lack of complete court rolls between 1283 and 1365, information about the work being done in the manor is sketchy. However,

---

[76] BL 9002.

we can be sure that many tenants kept pigs. The accounts of 1329-30 include £2 6s 9d received for pannage in the Homwode. At a penny a pig, this suggests that at least 561 pigs were kept on the manor, although the sum probably includes other beasts being allowed to graze. Trespass cases provide some further evidence for the kind of farming being practised. As we have seen, William de Brugges was growing rye, which had been illegally hoed and trampled. Robert Mum and Peter at Watere had pigs which got loose on the earl's land, as did two cows belonging to William Bacheler and one belonging to Peter Spicer. Thomas Compedon grazed sixteen beasts in the earl's pasture, while Robert Kynge and Richard at Lote obviously had flocks of sheep because they were fined for grazing them in the earl's demesne and then moving them on so they manured their own land instead of his. The clay soil continued to cause problems: Adam Coleman gave the earl 12d for permission to make a ditch five feet wide and 25 perches long, which would encroach on the Homwode. This must have been to aid drainage on his land.

For the first time, we have details of the kind of bread being made in Dorking. Regulated by the same assize as the sales of ale, bread was sold for either a farthing or a halfpenny: the weight of the loaf varied depending on the price of grain. The loaves available to the Dorking shopper included white bread or whole bread and wastelbread or simnel. Wastel and simnel were high quality loaves, made of very fine, white flour; the flour for simnel was boiled before baking (like a modern bagel). The cheaper form of

Baking bread
in an oven.

white bread was usually called cocket. Thomas Conygrove, Peter Kene, Richard Kene, Stephen Kentyng, Richard Muleward, Stephen Ophebbere, Christiana de Wadelshurst and William le Yonge were all fined in the 1340s for breaking the assize. We also know of a Dorking baker who plied his trade in London: known as 'Richard de Dorking', he was admitted to the Bakers Company in 1310.[77] A 'Richard le Baker' appears in the 1342 court roll, pursuing a debt owed by William Bachelere and accused of trespass by William de Brugges; if this were the London baker, he would have been rather long-lived, so perhaps this refers to either Richard Kene or Richard Muleward.

72 brewers were named in the court records that survive from the 1340s, of which nine were women. As usual, some were more prolific than others: Richard Alet, John Chapman, Robert Fisher, Richard Gilemyn, John at Ok, Rose Sepeld and Gilbert Tanner paid the fee more than once. Five men were named by the Walde aletasters: Robert at Bere, Robert Charesmore, Robert Clerk, Robert Pleystowe and Robert Upbroke. (The fact that they are all called Robert is a coincidence that nicely demonstrates the limited pool of Christian names.) Nineteen of the alesellers had paid the lay subsidy ten years before, so must have been fairly well-to-do, but it is difficult to decide who were the commercial brewers as opposed to the casual on such incomplete data.[78] The second names of some of the alesellers also provide evidence for other forms of employment on the manor; bearing in mind the usual proviso regarding 'surnames', we can surmise the presence of a carpenter, a clerk, a cooper, several fishmongers, a smith, a tailor and a tanner.

The church also offered employment opportunities. Evidence for the clerical careers of several Dorking men can be found in the registers of the bishops of Winchester. In March 1322/3, a sub-deacon called Robert Alarde

---

[77] Letter Book D, p.48.

[78] Those who paid were: Richard Brekespere, Adam Carpenter, John Couper, William le Fisher, William Fust, Gilbert Hichekoc, Alice Hurlewyne, Robert Noble, snr, William Ode, Henry Olyne, Henry Page, Robert Pleystowe, Peter Pruut, Henry Roper, Peter Spicer, Ralph Spicer, Thomas Taillur, Gilbert Tanner and Peter at Watere.

was recommended for the diaconate and priesthood.[79] Several acolytes were ordained as priests: Nicholas at Sonde in March 1324, a Master Roger in December 1325 and Thomas Wanton in February 1330.[80] A canon of Reigate priory called Brother Roger was ordained in March 1326/7 and a Brother Walter became a deacon in June 1327.[81] All these men were specified as being 'of Dorking'. We don't know if there was a school attached to the church in Dorking but it seems likely; clever boys in this period started their education locally before going on to the universities. A Roger de Dorking was particularly successful. He acted as an envoy of the archbishop of Canterbury and held a number of livings: in the 1340s he was rector of Chertham, in the Canterbury diocese, and a canon of Lichfield. He was subsequently presented with the canonries of St Laurence's in Romsey and of Bromyard in the Hereford diocese and, ultimately, the archdeaconry of Stafford.[82]

A bishop baptising a child.

[79] Sandele & Asserio registers, p.384 (523).
[80] Stratford register, vol II, pp.441, 453 & 509 (1474, 1489 & 1510).
[81] Stratford register, vol II, pp.468 & 476 (1489 & 1494).
[82] Petitions to the Pope, pp.131, 140, 158, 190 & 275.

The Church

On Corpus Christi day, a great procession wound through the town. At the front, the clergy carried the sacrament encased in a pyx of crystal, silver or gold. It was a solemn progress, accompanied by many candles and followed by the great and good of Dorking. Those they passed in the streets would kneel, the men bareheaded. The Feast of Corpus Christi was relatively new, having been introduced by Pope Urban IV in 1264 and relaunched in 1317. Created to honour the body of Christ and to celebrate the central mystery of the Eucharist, it became extremely popular, with specialist guilds being formed to organise the processions. It was held in early summer, on the Thursday after Trinity Sunday.

Of course, given the lack of local church records at this point, we can't be certain that there was a Corpus Christi procession in Dorking, although it seems likely. If it did take place, it would have been led by the vicar; in 1318, this was Henry de Habitone. He was followed by Thomas Everard, who then swapped benefices with John de Arderne. We have no further information about Henry or Thomas but John had previously been rector of Wakeley, in Hertfordshire; in 1324, he came to Dorking and Thomas went to Wakeley. John must have been well-regarded by the bishop, as he held a commission at penitentiary in Guildford deanery.[83] (This was an appointment where a priest represented the bishop, with power to absolve many offences.) John was succeeded by William de Blakelonde on 22 May 1349.[84]

Rather more information survives about the rectors of Dorking. John de Warenne, who had been in place since the 1290s, was not a particularly impressive incumbent. He held a number of other positions besides Dorking; as rector, he was not required to be resident in the parish but perhaps, being one of the earl's sons, he knew it was up the road from Reigate castle. Already in trouble for not storing produce on church grounds, between 1308 and 1313, he was being chased for a number of debts. He owed 25 marks to one Christiana, widow of John Seculer, which she pursued via the court of common pleas. As de Warenne was a cleric,

---

[83] Stratford register, vol I, p.173 (526).
[84] Stratford register, vol I, pp.283-4 (855).

the court had to work through the bishop of Winchester, Henry Woodlock. Unfortunately for Christiana, the bishop's servants tried and failed several times to find any goods at Dorking church on which her money could be raised because they were prevented from gaining access by the rector's bailiff. The bishop excommunicated de Warenne and his bailiff and the church was placed under an interdict but that wasn't enough to get the bishop off the hook. He had to ask the sheriff of Surrey to take the county force and get the goods or else appear before the king and Christiana to explain why he had been unable to carry out the court's mandate. Finally, at the end of December 1310, enough goods to cover the debt were sequestered by the sheriff's men and the bishop's servants, although finding someone to buy them proved difficult.[85]

What the people of Dorking made of all this is not recorded. The sight of the bishop's servants trying to get in to the church or the tithe barn and being seen off by the rector's bailiff must have been somewhat unedifying (if exciting), let alone the sheriff of Surrey arriving with an armed force to sort it out. Being under an interdict was more serious: no baptisms, marriages or funerals could take place until it was lifted. Regrettably, this was not the end of John de Warenne's indebtedness. He was subsequently had up before the court of common pleas for owing a debt of £5 and damages of £2 to a Master Elias of St Albans. Again, his bailiff resisted: he was now named as Roger and again excommunicated. Eventually, the money was raised and sent by bearers to the court.[86] The rector also owed £12 6s 8d to a Master James of Spain, who pursued the debt through the exchequer. The debt was described as 'long overdue' and the payment of it was equally tortuous. Firstly, £1 6s 8d was to be raised from the sale of goods already collected and four marks sent by bearer; apparently, no more goods were available. Then another £8 6s 8d worth of goods were sequestered, with the usual trouble finding buyers, and a subsequent attempt to raise the rest of the money failed because William of 'Gartone' (presumably Garston), serjeant of the rector, vigorously resisted the bishop's

---

[85] Woodlock register, vol II, pp.941, 946, 952, 960 & 962.
[86] Woodlock register, vol II, pp.993, 996-7 & 1010.

servants. He was excommunicated. Eventually, goods were taken to the value of the required £1 6s 8d.[87]

In 1322, John de Warenne was succeeded by John de Malmesbury, who held a number of ecclesiastical and government positions, travelling overseas on the king's business.[88] He only held the post for three years, exchanging benefices in 1325 with Robert de Balne, rector of Harthill in the diocese of York.[89] All three rectors were referred to as 'Master', signifying a university education.

Robert de Balne would be rector of Dorking until he died, at which point the church at Dorking and chapel at Ewekene were appropriated by Reigate Priory. This had been in the wind for some years: in 1329, the prior at Lewes was ordered to justify the £6 pension the priory received from Dorking.[90] He failed to do so. Subsequently, the canons of Reigate Priory petitioned for the appropriation, which was licensed by the king in 1334. Permission from the bishop took longer and it didn't come into force until November 1341, after the death of the rector.[91] It may also have been at this point that Capel became a separate parish from Dorking.

A Corpus Christi procession.

[87] Woodlock register, vol II, pp.1004-6, 1016 & 1021.
[88] CPR EdII, vol IV, pp.48 & 141.
[89] Stratford register, vol I, pp.308-9 (974).
[90] Stratford register, vol I, p.151 (469).
[91] CPR EdIII, vol III, p.9, Orleton register, pt I, fos 17r, 19v, 57v & pt 2, fo 90v & HRO DC/A2/23.

The Earl's Private Life

The current lord of the manor was John, grandson of the previous earl. Like his grandfather, he spent a fair bit of his time fighting the Scots, although he refused to go in 1313 and thus avoided the battle of Bannockburn. In 1324, he was appointed captain-general of a force raised for the relief of Aquitaine, under the command of the Earl of Kent. After Edward II was deposed, Edward III raised an army which defeated the Scots at Halidon Hill and restored John Balliol to the crown; Earl John was with the king and was thereafter repeatedly sent to Scotland and elsewhere.

The earl's personal life was somewhat tangled. He was married on the 25 May 1306 to Joan de Barre, grand-daughter of Edward I. The match was arranged by the king and enthusiastically taken up by the earl. Unfortunately, it was not a success. The earl was about twenty; Joan was ten or eleven, so she would have continued living in the royal household for several years. By 1309, something was wrong: the king gave the earl permission to make anyone he chose his heir, as long as he didn't disinherit any children he might have with Joan. In 1313, the king sent for Joan to come and live at his expense in London.

By this point, the earl was living with a lady called Maud. She was the widow of Sir Simon de Derby and daughter of Sir William de Nerford (in Norfolk), so was high-born and well-connected. In May 1313, the earl was threatened with excommunication because of his adultery but the king stepped in to prevent it. In 1316, the earl began a court case to divorce Joan; he offered her £200 a year and land worth 740 marks but, as none of the arguments he and Maud suggested held water, the case was thrown out. A council of nobles led by Thomas de Lancaster also condemned them, which led to a lengthy feud between the earl and de Lancaster. (Most of the fighting took place in Yorkshire so needn't concern us here.)

Meanwhile, the earl's family was growing. By 1316, two boys had been born to Maud and the earl surrendered his castles and manors in Surrey, Sussex and Wales to the king so that, when the king regranted them for his lifetime, it could be stipulated that his sons, John and Thomas, were his heirs.[92] (This is probably the John de Warenne who became rector of Dorking.) In the same year, the earl was excommunicated by the bishop of Chichester for adultery. By 1323, Maud had been granted some of the earl's lands in Norfolk, which later passed to one of their sons.

Unfortunately for Maud, the relationship then started to cool. In 1326, when the earl returned from the expedition to Aquitaine, he travelled with his wife, Joan. The earl again surrendered his land in Surrey, Sussex and Wales to the king, so that it could be returned to him and Joan. On their deaths, it would then pass to Edmund, Earl of Arundel, and his family as Earl John had no legitimate heirs.[93]   In 1327, John and Joan both received a safe conduct from the king to travel together. However, Joan then returned to France with her whole household in 1331. Maud was not happy about being discarded and tried to bring a case against the earl. She died sometime before 22 November 1345.

The reason that Maud was cast off and Joan went back to France seems to be that the earl met Isabelle Holland, another well-born lady who became his mistress. She was much younger than him, having been born around 1320. This relationship led the earl to try again to divorce his wife; he managed to get a papal bull declaring the marriage invalid but the English bishops ignored it. Then, in 1344, the pope commanded him to treat his wife with 'marital affection' and absolved him of any wrongdoing regarding a supposed adultery with the king's sister (don't ask). The earl again surrendered his castles and manors in Surrey, Sussex and Wales and Edward III re-granted them to the earl and the legitimate heirs of his body. Unfortunately, this charter disinherited his nephew, Richard, Earl of Arundel, who complained and had it cancelled.[94]

On 13 October 1346, the earl was exempted from attending Parliament on account of his being 'too feeble to work'. His health may have been failing for a while: two years earlier, the pope agreed that his confessor could give him plenary remission at the hour of his death.[95] He died at the end of June

[92] CCR Ed II, vol II, p.347.
[93] CPR EdII, vol V, pp.271-2 & CCR Ed II, vol IV, p.573.
[94] CPR EdIII, vol VII, p.221 & CPR EdIII vol VIII, p.327.
[95] Papal Register, vol III, p.115.

1347 and was buried at Lewes. In his will, he left various bequests to Isabelle Holland and five of his children; his widow, Joan, received nothing. However, she did have a life interest in the castles and manors in Surrey, Sussex and Wales, which included Dorking, Betchworth and Reigate. As she lived abroad, she appointed attorneys to manage her affairs. [96]

The seal of John, Earl de Warenne.

---

[96] All information on the earl's love-life is derived from Kathryn Warner's blogpost entitled 'the Amatory Adventures of John de Warenne'. Without it, the author would not have got to the bottom of the various surrenders and re-grants of the earl's land, let alone how many children he had and by whom.

The Wider World

The Scottish and French wars may have involved a number of men from Dorking. Evidence from the London records shows that in 1320-22 the mayor, aldermen and commonalty of London agreed to provide 200 armed foot-soldiers for the current conflict.[97] Every citizen of 'the more powerful and better class' was tasked with finding one armed soldier and the list of such citizens includes a 'Richard de Dorkyngge'. The foot-soldiers they recruited were also named and include a 'Richard Tailleboys'. Tayleboys (spelled a number of different ways) is a name which occurs in several Dorking records, so perhaps Richard the London citizen came back to Dorking to find his man. Ten years later, in 1334, the City paid Edmund Flambard, a knight of Kent, to raise 100 horsemen and 100 footsoldiers. Among the horsemen were Thomas and Robert de Ansty. Among the footsoldiers was Peter Lovel. We can't be certain that these were Dorking men but the names are local.[98] (Also, the next man in the list after Peter Lovel was a John de Guldeford.) In 1339, the earl himself held a commission to raise troops in Surrey for the new war in France.[99]

The earl was one of the noblemen who had revolted against the Despensers' influence over Edward II. In 1321, he was pardoned along with nineteen of his men. Three of these men were from Dorking: Maurice de Dorking, Robert Weston and William Duuk.[100] It seems likely that 'Maurice de Dorking' is the man known to us as Maurice de Ewekene. Robert Weston was constable of Reigate in 1329-30. No further information survives about William Duuk, although a Robert Duk appears in the 1344-5 court roll as an aleseller.

The connections between London and Dorking were still strong. In 1344, a survey was taken of all the Thames-side wards. From this, we learn that two of the little streets in Vintry Ward that ran down to the river were called 'Dorkynggeslane' and 'Reygateslane'.[101] Quite why the men of Dorking and

---

[97] Letter Book E, p.93.
[98] Letter Book E, pp.2-3.
[99] CCR EdIII, vol V, p.54.
[100] CPR EdII, vol IV, p.17.
[101] Liber Custumarum, p.450.

of Reigate should have streets named for them in the Vintry is a mystery but there do seem to have been various connections with the place. The 1292 Subsidy Roll for Vintry Ward includes two names which may have links to Dorking: Robert le Mareschal, a surgeon who also appeared in the 1282-3 manor court roll, and Simon le Seler, who could be related to Elias le Seler, one of the alesellers who had a stall in Dorking market.[102] When, in 1308, an inquiry into the property of a wealthy vintner called Ralph Hardel took place, a John de Dorking served as one of the jurors.[103] Another link lies in the fact that Idonia, widow of one Robert de Dorking, citizen of London, subsequently married Walter Turk, fishmonger and mayor, who lived in Vintry Ward.[104]

Richard de Dorking was a corndealer. He appeared in the Queenhithe subsidy roll in 1292 but also had a wharf in Vintry ward.[105] In 1302, he witnessed a quitrent in which all the people involved were Vintry residents. He also witnessed an aquittance by a burgess of Bordeaux to Ralph de Honilane, vintner.[106] In his will, Richard left his wife Matilda a number of lands and tenements, including one in the parish of St Martin in the Vintry, with a view to maintaining a chantry for his soul in the said church for five years after his death.[107] Corndealers were very important for the war effort. In 1322/3, William de Dorking was one of the corndealers tasked with checking the quality of wheat and flour ready to be shipped from London to Scotland.[108] He was married to Agnes and guardian to the children of Henry de Merlawe (her first husband), as well as executor of the will of one of the aldermen. He and Agnes were living in Castle Baynard ward in 1319 and he seems to have known Richard, as the latter stood surety for William regarding the guardianship.[109]

---

[102] Two Early London Subsidy Rolls, pp.181-6.
[103] Letter Book C, p.241.
[104] Letter Book E, p.246 & Calendar of Wills, pt 1, p.330 (26).
[105] Two Early London Subsidy Rolls, pp.147-152 & Coroners Roll, p.127 (41).
[106] Letter Book B, p.185 & Letter Book C, p.189.
[107] Calendar of Wills, pt 1, p.294 (121).
[108] PRO SC 8/261/13039.
[109] Letter Book E, pp.91 & 181.

Two more familiar names come up in the London records at this time. Walter Mum was described as a 'merchant of Surrey'; he was obviously doing business at a high level, because, in 1314, he owed 104s (£5 4s) to a Philip de Fifehead, merchant of London, for goods sold retail and received by Walter from Philip.[110] As we have seen, Walter held property in Dorking and was presumably related to the Juliana Mum who appeared in the lay subsidy and the Richard and Robert Mum who were both named in the 1340s court rolls. Another familiar name is that of John Stub, who held land on the manor between Godwyns and the Innome and paid the lay subsidy alongside Ralph Stub. In 1346, John owed £60 to John de Slappele, a woodmonger of London.[111]

The Black Death struck England in autumn 1348. Arriving first at southern ports, it spread quickly, reaching London at the beginning of November. We do not know when the first plague death occurred in Dorking and we have no direct evidence for the impact of the pestilence on the manor; no Dorking court rolls survive for the period and nor do any Surrey wills. Given that the national death toll is estimated as being at least 40% of the population, we might expect something similar in Dorking, particularly as the manor was only a day's journey from London. However, the pestilence didn't strike evenly. Some villages were almost wiped out, while other locations remained relatively untouched.

There is some indirect evidence for the Black Death's local impact. The first example lies in the fact that, when William de Blakelond became vicar on 22 May 1349, the position was vacant.[112] Had John de Arderne died of the plague? Clergy were often victims because their role brought them into close contact with the suffering and dying; the number of empty benefices in Surrey increased tenfold during the plague year.[113] The church responded by promoting clergy more rapidly than usual. Walter Chapman of Merrow was confirmed as sub-deacon on the 7th March, as deacon on the 18th March and as priest on the 6th June, all in 1349. He was one of many

---

[110] PRO C241/82/115.
[111] PRO C241/123/120.
[112] Edington register, pt 1, p.84 (532).
[113] VCH Surrey, vol IV, p.418.

going through the same process; in the 1360s, he would become vicar of Dorking.[114]   A second piece of evidence is provided by a deed dated 29 January 1348/9. In it, Richard at Sonde granted certain lands and tenements, plus 'all the goods and chattels moveable and immoveable in the aforesaid tenements', to Matilda, widow of a Roger de Mucforthe. The deed specifies that on Matilda's death, the property should pass to her daughter, Lore; so far, so straightforward. Then it continues: "... should the said Lore die with heirs unnamed all the said lands ... shall remain to Isabelle daughter of Richard at Forthe of Send. And in the event of the said Isabelle dying with heirs unnamed all the said lands shall remain for ever to Henry my son and his heirs ... And should the said Henry die with heirs unnamed ... all the said lands shall remain for ever to my son Richard."[115] Why was Richard at Sonde so concerned about all these young people dying intestate? Why were the goods and chattels also included, unless the inhabitants no longer needed them? Can the impact of the pestilence be seen in this document?

Meanwhile, the routine business of the church went on despite the terrible situation.   In September 1349, John Spicer of Dorking was summoned to be examined by the archdeacon of Surrey. Unfortunately, we don't know anything more about him or what he had done to attract the attention of the religious authorities.[116]

The population of England bounced back surprisingly quickly in the immediate aftermath of the Black Death. However, further episodes of plague in 1361 and thereafter led to long-term decline in numbers. The population didn't recover until the 16thC.

---

[114] Edington Register, pt 2, pp.138, 143 & 146 (770, 776 & 784).
[115] BL 18645.
[116] Papal Registers, vol III, p.325.

N

Dorking
town

Homwode

Ewekene / Capel

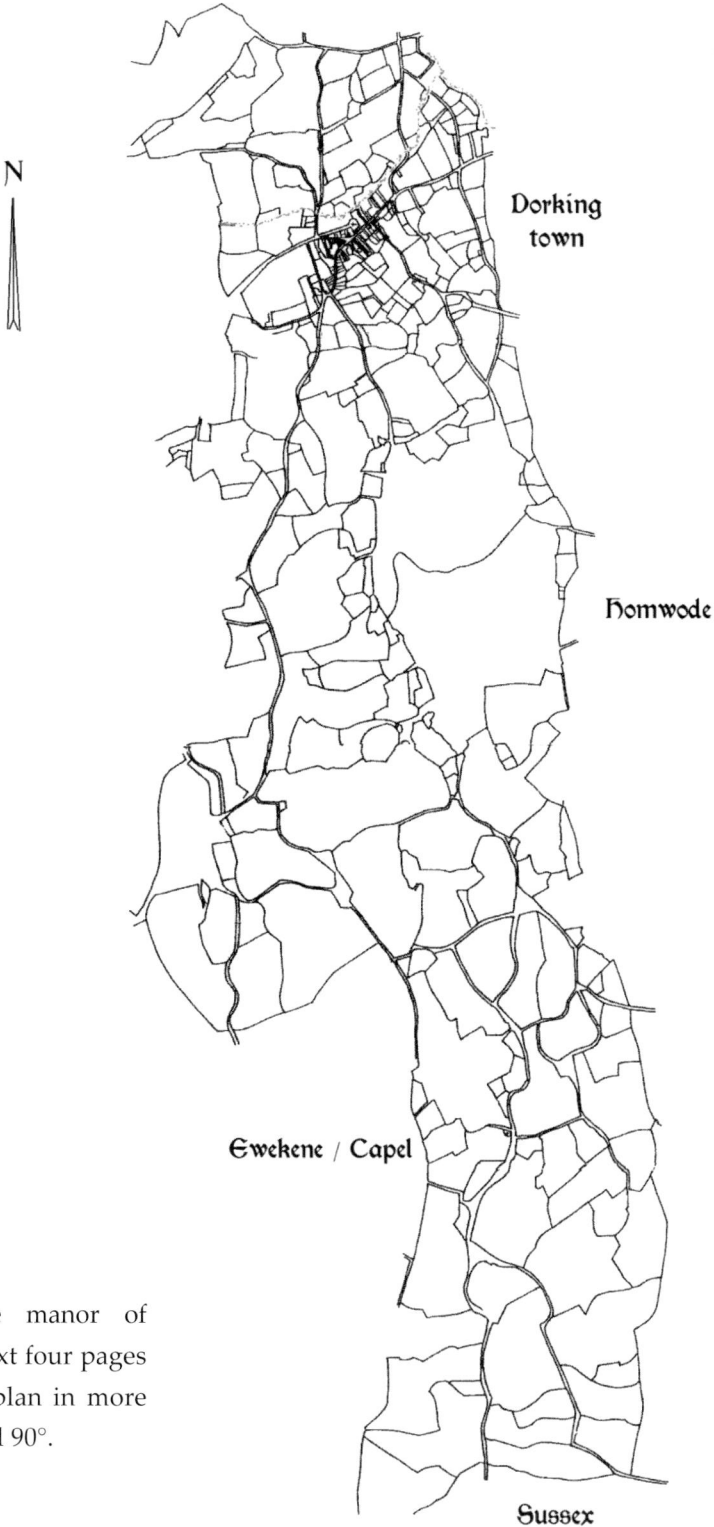

A plan of the manor of
Dorking. The next four pages
show the same plan in more
detail and rotated 90°.

Sussex

The Manor of Dorking during the late 13th to late 14th centuries

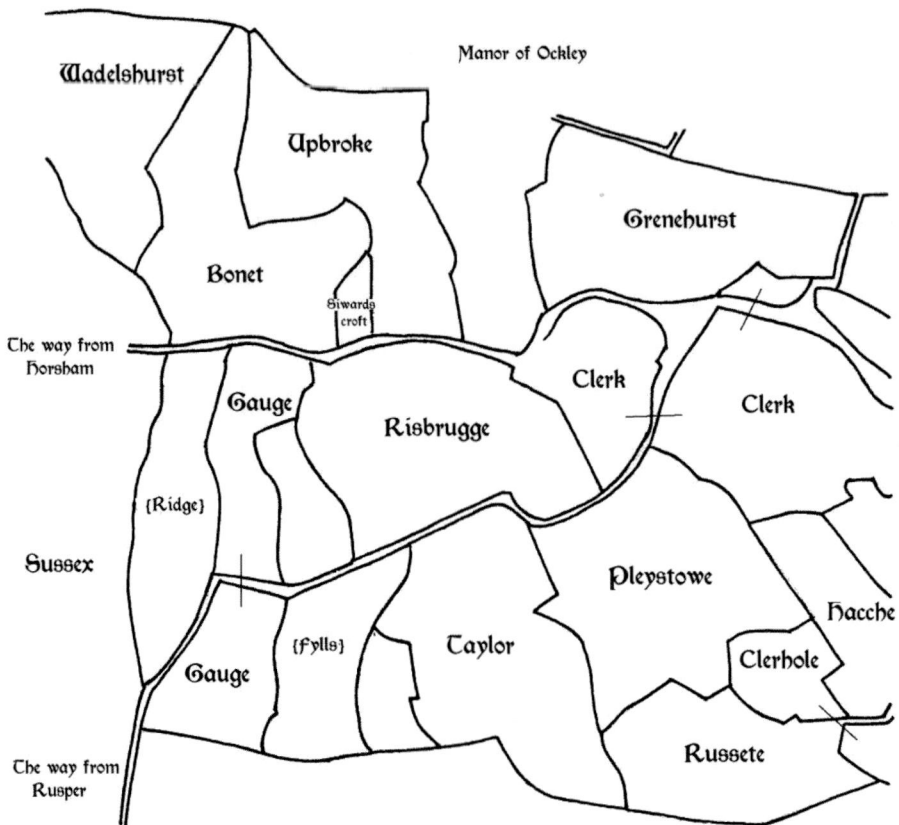

N

Wadelshurst

Manor of Ockley

Upbroke

Greneburst

Bonet

Siwards croft

The way from Horsham

Clerk

Clerk

Gauge

Risbrugge

{Ridge}

Sussex

Pleystowe

Hacche

{Fylls}

Taylor

Clerhole

Gauge

Russete

The way from Rusper

Brokwick

Lythe

Coldharbour

Manor of Milton

Charesmore

Waterdene

Langshete

{Kitlands}

Ansty

Bere

Manor of Milton

Manor of Ockley

{Arnolds}

Brekespere

Ewekene

Rugge

Bonet Charesmore

Sprot

Tournour

Bruggesulle

Smith

Glebe land

Helde

Garston

Thurbarn

Hulle

Ketleas

Brouman

Mesbroke

Clerhole

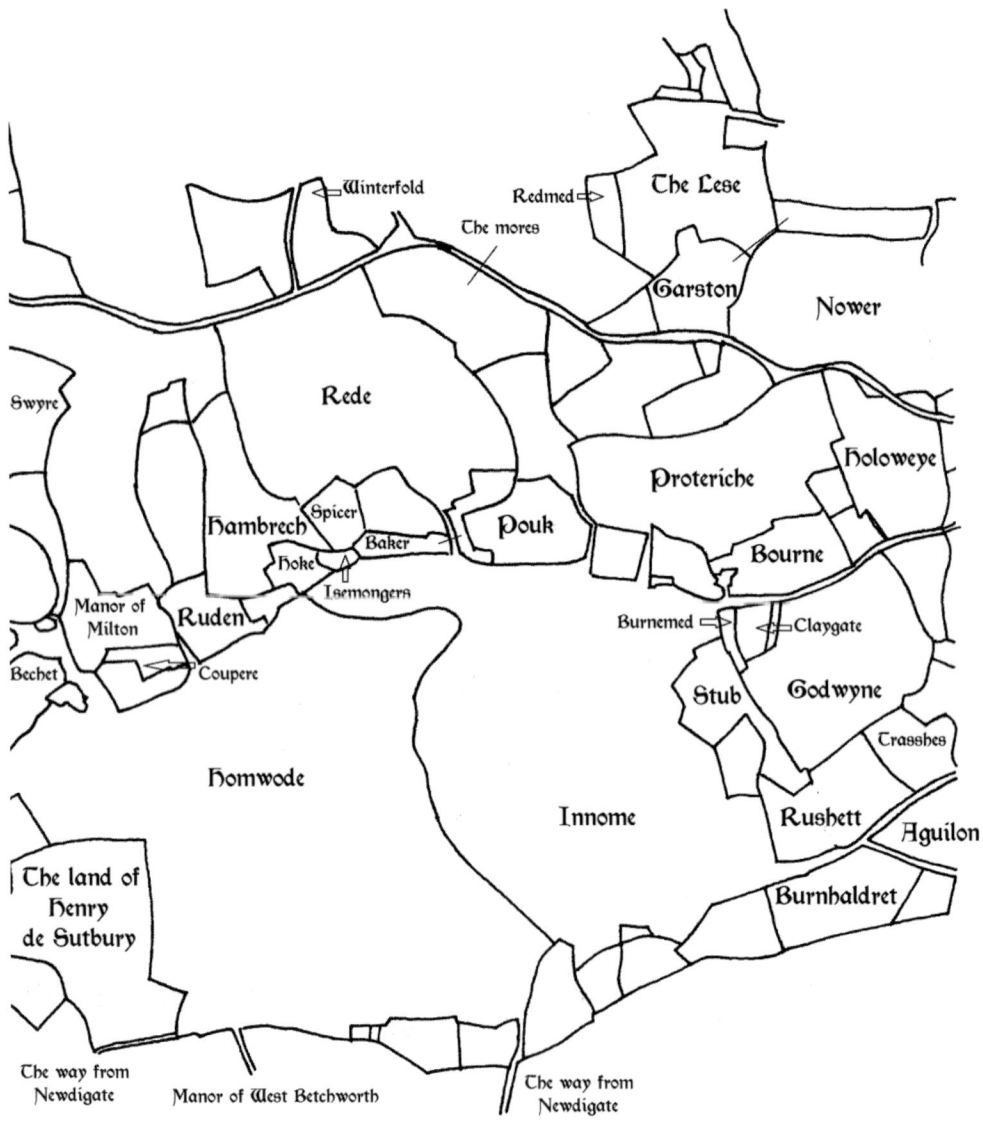

Winterfold

Redmed

The Lese

The mores

Swyre

Rede

Garston

Nower

Proteriche

Holoweye

Spicer

Hambrech

Baker

Pouk

Bourne

Hoke

Isemongers

Burnemed

Claygate

Manor of
Milton

Ruden

Bechet

Coupere

Stub

Godwyne

Crasshes

Homwode

Innome

Rushett

Aguilon

The land of
Henry
de Sutbury

Burnhaldret

Manor of Milton

Snokes bacche

Denbies

Ashcombe

Hamsted

Buryfeld

Glebe land

Sonde

Dorking Downs

Ruden

Manor of Mickleham

Manor of Bradley

Derry feld

Buryhill

Osward

North brook

Noble

Summers Leas

Mapeldrefeld

Medmulle

Bovetoune

Mum

Parrok

Demesne land

Stoney lond

The way from Reigate

Cotman dene

Pipfelde

Tebeham

Lythiere

Sket

Forstrode

Shiplond

Redleve

Water dene

Mill crofts

Heghe lond

Dibden Deth

Chert

Aguilon

Oggestole

Scale 3″ to 1 mile approx

83

Between the Black Death and the Peasants' Revolt: 1350-1380

On the 9th February 1365/6, the freeholders and tenants living in the manor of Dorking came to swear fealty to their new lord. Richard, Earl of Arundel, had inherited the title of Earl of Surrey from his uncle in 1347. As the late earl's lands in Surrey, Sussex and Wales had been granted to his widow for her lifetime, it was only when Joan de Barre died in 1361 that Richard came into this part of his inheritance.

The court roll records that forty-seven freeholders and all the customary tenants and cottars came to the manor court to swear the oath of allegiance. However, when these men knelt and placed their hands into those of the earl's steward, it was not to Earl Richard that they swore fealty. Instead, the new lord of the manor comprised nineteen men, ranging from the Duke of Lancaster (otherwise known as John of Gaunt) and the Earl of Hereford (Humphrey de Bohun), through ten other knights and six gentlemen.[117] Four further manor courts were held in their names and then, on the 1st June, Earl Richard was reinstated as lord of the manor. There was no swearing ceremony that day.

What was going on? Great lords often enfeoffed their land to the king, if they were going overseas or to war or they wanted to secure the inheritance in a particular direction. As seen previously, Earl John surrendered his land in Surrey, Sussex and Wales to the king several times in response to changes in his relationships, almost disinheriting his nephew in the process. In August 1360, Earl Richard sought assurance from the king that he would be able to enter all the castles, manors, lands, knight's fees and advowsons which were held by Joan de Barre, without having to go through the usual channels. He received permission so to do and the situation was ratified in December 1361.[118]

Six weeks later, the earl sought a licence to surrender his property to the king, via the abovementioned nineteen men; in April, everything was returned to Richard and his wife, Eleanor, for their lifetimes, with the

---

[117] See Appendix C for the list of enfeoffees and the freeholders of Dorking manor. The customary tenants and cottars were not named.
[118] CPR EdIII, vol XI, pp.458-9 & CPR EdIII, vol XII, p.123.

remainder to their sons in succession.[119]   Not only was this transaction recorded among the Patent Rolls (as one would expect), it also appeared in the records known as 'feet of fines'.   These are a particularly useful set of documents, beginning in the 12[th]C and continuing until the nineteenth, which recorded property deals through the fiction of a dispute. The details were copied out three times on one piece of parchment, then divided up: one copy was given to each party and the bottom of the document (the foot of the fine) was stored at the royal court, thus providing a central record of the transaction.   Earl Richard's surrender of his land in Surrey, Sussex and Wales was recorded on the 19th April 1366 and the return of all this property appears in the next foot of fine, dated 3rd May 1366. The earl should have paid £200 for the process but the king waived the fees.[120]

After his experience twenty years earlier, when he had to appeal to the king to secure his inheritance, it seems likely that the earl wanted to make absolutely sure that his property was secure.   However, if the whole business were a legal fiction to get everything down on parchment, why did the Dorking freeholders and tenants have to turn up at the manor court and swear fealty to these nineteen new lords, only to have the situation reversed a few weeks later?

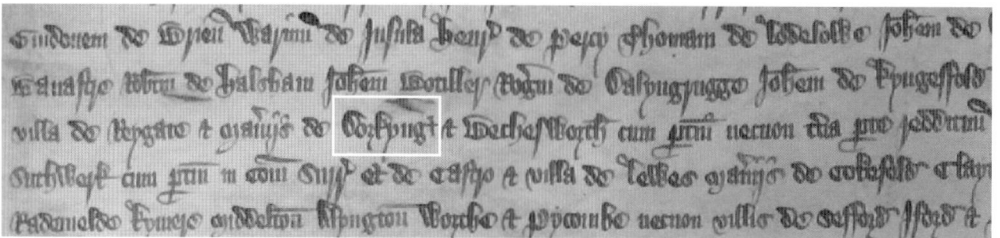

An extract from the foot of fine describing the earl's property.
'Dorking' is highlighted.

---

[119] CPR Ed III, vol XIII, pp.198 & 237-8.
[120] Pedes Finium, p.221 (663 & 664) & CPR EdIII, vol XIII, p.239.

At the Manor Court

Apart from this, the business of the manor court carried on as normal. Attendance seems to have held up; in 1365, only two people paid to be excused until the following Michaelmas. They were John Carpenter and Matilda, the daughter of Richard Gylemyn, a butcher and an aleseller in Estborough.[121] Eight people were essoined for suit of court during the year, most of them two or three times (the maximum allowed). This is significantly fewer than in 1282-3. No accounts survive for 1365-6 but, ten years later, it was recorded that 2s 3d was spent on buying parchment for the court rolls. This is the first time we get a glimpse of the bureaucracy supporting the manor court.

There were only twelve cases of debt pursued during this manorial year, fewer than in the partial records of the 1340s. Three were handled by an attorney called John Barbour, including one between William Paton of Leatherhead and John Athelingham of Westcote; one wonders why it was heard in the Dorking court. Ralph at Heghlond and William Anstye, the beadles, got into trouble several times because they didn't present the people required for these debt cases to proceed.

In contrast, cases of trespass were on the rise. Numbers of livestock on the manor had increased and this seems to have led to more incidents of trespass and a greater concern regarding the maintenance of hedges. The reeve brought to the attention of the court several cases of beasts roaming where they shouldn't. Thomas Rede was cited when two of his cows got into the Hambrech, which bordered his land. The Hambrech and the nearby Ruden and Swyre seem to have been particularly vulnerable to trespass: Hugh Netelfolde and John at Chert each had swine loose in the Hambrech, while John Wodeward's swine got out in the Ruden. William Ansty was fined 6d because his animals got into the Swyre; his property was right next door and he was also indicted for having an insufficient enclosure. John Smyth was fined for the same offence at the Hambrech. In total, the earl brought twenty-five cases against twenty individuals for allowing their animals to stray into his oats, barley or corn. Most involved

---

[121] The text says 'Gamelyn' but this surname seems to have been particularly difficult to spell.

one or two animals, predominately swine or horses, but the earl's pasture was also invaded by five bullocks belonging to Richard Shepherd. The fines were usually between 2d and 4d, although John Coker was fined half a mark for the damage his pig did among the earl's barley.

John Hotte, Hugh at Sonde, Thomas Tournour and John Wodeward were all fined 2d for throwing down an enclosure in Dorking, contrary to the earl's prohibition. Without knowing where this incident took place, it's difficult to interpret what went on. However, they weren't the only hedge-breakers: John (son of William Carpenter), Juliana (servant of Thomas Tournour) and Margery (servant of Peter Bonet) were all cited for the same offence. William Carpenter stood as pledge for his son John and Peter Bonet for his servant Margery; one hopes they paid the fines of their dependants. As well as maintaining hedges, one of the burdens on property holders near major roads was the requirement to keep the land on each side clear, in accordance with the Statute of Winton. This responsibility applied equally to freeholders and to customary tenants: in the 1365-6 court roll, Robert at Risbrugge was cited for his tenancy at Risbrugge, as were William at Churche (for Spottisfeld), Robert de Weston (for Puppemulle) and William Drynkewater, Thomas Latyn and John Masoun (all for Marlynpulte). The fines varied between 3d, 6d or 12d, presumably depending on how overgrown the land was. Unfortunately, we don't know exactly where these fields were.

Trespass wasn't only a problem for the earl: seventeen private individuals brought similar cases. Robert de Weston was the most vigilant (or unlucky), accusing seven of his neighbours. John Wodeward's pigs were digging his pasture and destroying his herbage. Richard at Sonde and Richard Tepeham allowed their swine to get into his meadow, while Alan at Nabrette, Hugh Netelfolde and Hugh at Sonde allowed three cattle, one horse and one mare respectively into his barley. John Cotham also let his swine get into Robert's corn. The baker and brewer John Kene brought four cases, three about a cow in his barley and one about a horse in his corn, which must have had an impact on his business. One wonders what lay behind Richard at Sonde's accusation that Hugh at Sonde had allowed ten bullocks to trespass in his corn. The men must have been related but obviously couldn't sort it out in private. Two cases of trespass involved sheep, of which there were many more on the manor. Hugh Netelfolde made several accusations against Walter Peyter, including that he and a member of his household had driven ten sheep into his (Hugh's) pasture. Walter denied it and the matter was settled out of court. Meanwhile, John Smyth accused William Mum of trespass by sheep in his oats.

Most of those cited for trespass only appeared once or twice but there were a few serial offenders. The aforementioned Hugh at Sonde was also accused by the earl and by Robert de Weston. Laurence Ingylby was cited three times, as was Hugh Netelfolde, while John Wodeward was twice accused by the earl, once by Robert de Weston and once by Thomas Ashcombe. One unusual case was raised at the View of Frankpledge, when a jury of twelve reported on trespass by pullets belonging to John A Neve on the land of William Noble. The chickens had apparently been seized by William and unjustly hidden. In November, John brought a claim against William, alleging that he and a member of his household had killed and carried off three hens and twenty-three poultry from a croft called Cotberdylhaugh. (William held the croft in villeinage from the earl; we don't know exactly where it was.) William denied the charge and was supported by two pledges. The following January, William waged his law three-handed: he swore his innocence on oath, supported by three other oathmakers. John was fined for making a false complaint and, in February, William brought a case against him, alleging that the latter's swine and hens had destroyed Cotberdylhaugh. John denied it and waged his law three-

Weeding the crops.

handed. The parties were given a day to sort it out and, it seems, settled the matter out of court.

The earl continued to have a problem with illegal hunting. Seven people were required to answer the charge of killing a hare in his warren, including the vicar (Walter Chapman) and a woman (Matilda, daughter of Richard Gylemyn). The other five accused were William Coupere, John Donnere, Nicholas de Henle, Hugh at Sonde and Adam Whytyng. The vicar was acquitted, being supported by the whole homage, and we don't know what happened to the charge against Matilda; a subsequent list of eight people fined 12d each for killing a hare didn't include her but did include the abovenamed five, plus John Bymysay, Thomas Fust and Richard Tepeham. Given the status of some of those involved, this sounds like organised hare-coursing rather than hunting for the pot. The earl had obviously issued an order requiring hunting dogs to be kept on a lead: Ralph at Heghlond, Adam at Homwode, Peter Kynge, John Ode and Roger Yonge were acquitted but seventeen others were asked to come to court and explain why they kept dogs without collars, running the risk of a 5s fine.[122]

Ferrets were also in use on the manor; we know this because the warrener presented one to the manor court as 'weif'. This signified abandoned goods which, if they remained unclaimed, would be awarded to

Returning from the hunt with greyhounds.

---

[122] Their names were: John A Neve, John de Balne, Peter Bonet, John Bymysay, John Coker, John Donnere, John Flecchere, Thomas Noble, John Oseward, Hugh at Sonde, Richard at Sonde, Juliana Spicer, Richard Suel, John Tannere, Thomas Tournour, John Wodeward and Adam Whytyng.

the earl by the steward. As well as the aforementioned ferret, six colts, five ewes and a black horse were 'proclaimed in town, market and church' before being declared as weif. The ferret was sold for 2s and John Coker took the ewes, for which he was summoned to explain himself at the next court. One of the colts turned out to belong to Walter Peyter; the other five were assigned to the earl as weif, with three being sold and two ending up in the earl's store.

The longest-running weif case involved seven ells of scarlet cloth. 'Scarlet' was the highest quality woollen fabric, teased and sheared on both sides after fulling until it was smooth as silk. It might then be dyed with the most expensive red dye (made from the Kermes beetle) but not always; 'scarlet' came to mean the colour but, at this point, signified the cloth. Scarlet was very expensive: the seven ells found in Dorking were valued at the end of the year at seven marks (£4 13s 4d). For comparison, the year before, the Black Prince spent £18 13s 4d on a whole cloth of scarlet to give to his household knights at Christmas. Seven ells of fabric was enough to make a long gown or robe but, according to the most recent sumptuary law of 1363, scarlet could only be worn by the wealthiest class of knights, those worth over 500 marks per annum.[123]

Who in Dorking could have lost seven ells of scarlet? The cloth was presented at the manor court by Ralph de Heghlond, beadle for Dorking, but he gave no details as to where it was found. There were three weavers and three tailors in Dorking, plus Laurence Ingylby, the fuller. None of these men would have produced such expensive fabric without a commission but who would have placed such an order? Whatever the background, someone must have lost a lot of money when the scarlet cloth landed in the hands of the authorities.

---

[123] Silverman (2001), pp. 29-30, 51 & 62-3.

Trouble and Strife

The View of Frankpledge held on Thursday, 1ˢᵗ October 1365 included a substantial list of violent interactions. In Waldeborough, John Bruggesulle assaulted John Hunte, who raised the hue and cry against him, while in Foreignborough, John Cotham drew blood from Mabel at Flusshe. Both these assailants were fined 6d. Things were even more lively in the town. The Chippingborough tithing reported six assaults: John Hotte on John Suel, William Motoun on Adam Wadelshurst, William Noble, snr on John Kene, jnr, Adam Whytyng on William Carpenter and Agnes, the wife of Matthew Taillour, on Juliana Thekeman; Agnes also drew blood. The hue and cry was raised in all cases and the fines were sixpence. Unfortunately, the detailed recording of former years was no longer practised, so we don't know what caused any of this trouble.

Even more seriously, Henry Sherewynd assaulted Richard Skinner when he was keeping the night watch in accordance with the Statute of Winton. Henry was fined 11d for this attack on officialdom. The Statute had been passed in 1285 in order to reform the system of watch and ward. It revived royal jurisdiction in local courts and required the hue and cry to be raised by the whole hundred. (This is the first time we've seen the hue and cry in action in Dorking because the 1282-3 roll was too early and those from the 1340s are incomplete.) In Dorking, the headborough and tithing of Chipping and East boroughs all got into trouble for not keeping the watch according to the Statute; the headboroughs were John Chapman for Chippingborough and Roger Yonge for Estborough. The Watch only applied in town, so Stephen at Mesbroke (Waldeborough) and John Ashcombe (Foreignborough) didn't have to worry. However, John did have to explain why Stephen at Holeweye was in his tithing but 'acting outside the assize'. Stephen paid a fine to leave Waldeborough and join Foreignborough, which may explain the confusion.

In Estborough, John Jolyfbon was fined 12d because he unjustly raised the hue and cry upon John Syre. There were four cases of violence in this borough. Margery, wife of Richard Skynnere, assaulted Alice, wife of Henry Oslak; both women seem to have evaded appearing in court, as their pledges were fined for not bringing the women in. Meanwhile, Rose, wife of Simon Aylward, assaulted Sibile, tenant of Ralph at Heghlond and drew blood. Sibile justly raised the hue and cry upon her. The other two cases of violence involved male assailants, when Walter Skamaill assaulted William Clerk and John at Medende assaulted Matthew Taillour. All the accused were fined 6d. Walter Skamaill was a respectable businessman, involved in trade with London merchants, so why he was involved in an altercation in the town is unclear. Rose and Sibil were also fined 3d for being common scolds (Lat *cogarilator*), as was Juliana Drynkewater. Such behaviour wasn't restricted to women: in Chippingborough, William Noble was fined for the same offence. Whether they ended up in the cucking-stool is unrecorded.

Another two cases of violence were described at the manor court held after the View of Frankpledge. In May, it was reported that John Kyngenho of Mickleham had maliciously beaten and badly hurt John, the son of John Upbroke, and also held in scorn and contempt the late Adam Brokere. Damages were set high at 100s and John Kyngenho was required to come to court to answer the charge; when he did so on the 1st June, he didn't deny the beating but said that he had chastised John Upbroke without hurting him. John Kyngenho obviously felt he had a strong case because he waged his law twelve-handed, bringing twelve oathmakers to swear to his innocence. On the 22nd June, John and his pledges appeared in court and he was acquitted. The second case was reported in June, when Richard Smyth brought an accusation against Henry Oslak for beating and wounding him, which Henry denied.

A fight! Most fights in Dorking seem not to have involved weapons.

The Demesne

Joan de Barre, widow of the previous earl, had spent most of her time in her native France, appointing attorneys to manage her affairs in England. In Dorking, the management of the manor seems to have undergone something of a decline during this period and the 1365-6 court roll shows some evidence of the new earl's officials catching up with the tenants. For a start, the regulations governing the grazing of animals on the Homwode were tightened when, at the beginning of the court year, Robert Gylmyn and many other tenants were fined 13s 6d for letting their animals graze outside the permitted period. In November, a report from the warrener was presented and a long list of all those who paid pannage, plus a much shorter list of those paying to graze other animals, was attached to the court roll. The entry included the names of the relevant tenants (freehold and customary), the numbers of pigs, cattle, mares or ewes being grazed and the amounts paid.[124] All this extra detail is unusual: most of the time, the amount of money received was recorded in the court roll and in the reeve's accounts without any additional information. The reeve took 24s 4d in total that year.

The status of customary land came up several times. In June, Thomas Rede was accused of selling beeches and oaks without permission. He was required to come to the next court to answer the charge but, by then, the issue seems to have widened: the whole homage was told to go

Knocking acorns down for the pigs to eat.

---

[124] See Appendix D.

and look at all the customary land and tenements in the demesne of Dorking and report any 'waste' to the steward at the next court, on penalty of 100s. In September, the homage reported that Hugh Netelfolde held a piece of customary land but had not sworn fealty for it and had made 'waste' on it to damages of 10s. Thomas Rede was found to have destroyed woods (damages of 40d), as had Nicholas at Hambrech (damages of half a mark). Hugh, Thomas and Nicholas were told to come to the next court to respond to the charges.

Hugh had already given the earl a fine of half a mark and sworn fealty for a tenement held in villeinage; perhaps he thought he would get away without doing so for this piece of land. The temptation to avoid official notice must have been strong, given that it cost John Harm 40d to gain permission to lease one piece of customary land at the Garston to Henry at Sonde. In another case, Walter Baker was summoned to show how he acquired three rods of customary land from Thomas Rede and the whole homage was distrained for concealing the alienation of the land. However, Walter presented the deed which showed it was actually free land and swore fealty for it.[125]

Richard at Lese was also caught up in this investigation into customary land. He held a piece of pasture and was asked to prove how he came into it and by what service he held it. Richard asked for the Extent to be examined, by which method he proved that he held the land freely. However, he had to pay half a mark for the document search. (The Extent shows that Agnes, widow of Richard at Lese, had acquired an acre of pasture in the time of Walter Bacheler, steward in 1299-1300. Perhaps she was the current Richard's grandmother.)

Problems also arose regarding two pieces of land which had dropped out of manorial control sixteen years previously. One was a meadow called Sywardislond, which was part of the Ewekene. In October, the whole homage presented that the land had been held by Lucy de Ewekene and that she was a bastard. (She had inherited it from Maurice de Ewekene, who was presumably her father.) When Lucy died without heirs, the land

---

[125] Also see BL 18663 where Walter Baker acquired another two acres next to Hambrech Lane from Juliana Spicer in March 1372.

should have come back into the earl's hand. Instead, Thomas Garland had acquired it: he was asked to show by what right he held the land and was charged with allowing it go to waste during the previous sixteen years, for which the earl claimed 100s in damages. However, at the November court, the steward affirmed that he had let seventeen acres to Thomas for 3s per acre, paid in the usual three tranches. Thomas then seems to have let the land to Thomas Plesshette, so he was also required to account for the earl's loss of revenue during the sixteen years.[126] Both men finally came to court in March and gave the earl 50s for damage done to the Sywardislond, payable the following Michaelmas.

The second such case involved Robert, Prior of Reigate, who held a portion of the customary tenement of Thomas Fust.[127] The prior was asked to show how he had right of entry to the land and was accused of unjustly keeping back 7½d a year in rent from the earl, currently in arrears for sixteen years. The prior was distrained twice but the matter hadn't been settled by the end of the court year, so we don't know what happened. If these acquisitions of part of the Fust tenement and the Sywardislond meadow took place sixteen years before 1365, that takes us back to 1349. Even without leaping to assumptions regarding the impact of the Black Death, it seems significant that these pieces of land slipped out of the steward's control during the years when Dorking's landlord was even more absent than usual.

One of the results of the Black Death was that landlords found it difficult to lease unproductive land or unattractive property, so tenancies fell vacant. There are some examples of this in the 1365-6 court roll: Peter de Hechurst's house, Richard Henhurst's tenement and John Motoun's tenement were all surrendered into the earl's hand, with the Hechurst house still unlet at the end of the year. One of the customary tenancies also fell vacant when John at Pleystowe died, remaining so during the rest of the court year.

---

[126] O'Fflahertie's transcription says eighteen years. The original roll is damaged at this point, so some of this information is derived from notes on the court rolls made in the 16thC.

[127] Perhaps the one next to Godfreys in Holowestret.

However, several heirs did claim their inheritance. Adam Belde's fifteen-year-old son, John, came and swore fealty for his father's free tenement and customary land. Both were worth 8d per annum to the earl; John paid heriot of an ox worth 20s and was asked to produce the deed by which his father held the freehold property. The heirs of John Chapman and of Rose Kene were also both called John. John Chapman paid no heriot but gave 6½d as a relief and swore fealty for his late father's messuage and curtilage. John Kene, son of Rose and the late Richard Kene, claimed a messuage and curtilage in the centre of town and a piece of land at Bury Hill. Again, no heriot was paid but he gave the 2s 2d relief and swore fealty for the property. Thomas Caas also gave 12d for the use of a piece of free land which had been the property of his wife, Matilda.

Walter Peyter was the reeve in 1365-6. His accounts don't survive but the court roll mentions some of the official business in which he was engaged. He sold underwood at the Lese to John Kene for 3s, wood in Middleinnome to Richard at Sonde for 23s 4d, herbage at Hambrech to Thomas Rede for half a mark and pasture in Redlevet to John Wodeward for 4d. Underwood next to the Medmulle and pannage in Burnhaldret were sold to Thomas Tournour for 10s and 11d respectively. The reeve also appeared several times in a private capacity. He was summoned for not keeping his tenement in good repair and, as we have seen, was also involved in a dispute with Hugh Netelfolde regarding trespass by his sheep in Hugh's pasture.

At the end of the court year, Walter leased the market and mills to Roger Yonge for sixteen marks; this must have been a renewal of his lease, as Roger had previously been fined 11d for unjustly levying tolls at the mill, with the headborough and tithing of Chippingborough fined 12d for concealing the fact. Roger was also fined for allowing his mare to trespass in the floodgates at one of the mills.

Roger was one of the freeholders who swore fealty at the February court and was headborough of the Estborough tithing. He was an aleseller, appearing at every court for breaking the assize, and was probably also a baker: a William le Yonge had appeared as such in the 1344-5 court roll and Roger is named as a baker in the 1380s. He obviously owned livestock because he paid pannage for one pig and a 2d fine when his draught animals trespassed in the earl's corn. There was also some kind of trouble with John A Neve; both men brought pleas of trespass against the other and were each fined 8d for not turning up to pursue their pleas. Roger was also one of the many residents required to explain why they kept hunting dogs without collars.

By 1376, the reeve was Thomas Rogger and it was he who presented the only set of accounts to survive between 1330 and the 1380s. Unfortunately, they only cover four months, from Michaelmas 1376 until the 24th January. Presumably, these were partial accounts presented for auditing. As the accounts cover the first third of the manorial year, only part of the revenue from customary tenants was recorded: 10s 10d in lieu of muck-spreading, 16s instead of 96 hens and the three payments related to the winter ploughing, threshing and harrowing of one plot of 13 acres and 2½ rods. The usual £4 tallage and 30s common fine taken at View of Frankpledge had also been received, as had the payment for pannage and the driving of beasts into the Homwode. In 1376, this amounted to 18s 8d, 5s 8d less than ten years earlier and signficantly down from 1329's impressive total of 46s 9d. However, receipts from the manor court were up. Including fines from View of Frankpledge, the first five courts of this manorial year had raised £6 7s 8d. In 1365, the first five courts plus View of Frankpledge made £5 18s 10d.

There were no sales of pasture or woods (because of the time of year) but sales of corn had taken place. Wheat was selling for 10s per quarter, oats for 2s 8d and barley for 8d. This is very much as expected after the Black Death, when a population with more spending power shunned cheaper forms of grain and chose to buy wheaten bread. Thus, the price of wheat went up, while that of oats and barley fell. For the first time, sales of rabbits from the earl's warren were recorded: 200 had been sold for £3 2s 6d, out of a total of 408. This was a significant improvement on 1365, when there was an enquiry by the constable and warrener into the lack of sales. The only wages mentioned in these partial accounts were paid to the warrener, who received 9s 8d. He was named in the 1365-6 court roll as Richard Lenkenore but may have been replaced by 1376.

Thomas Rogger's store account listed horses and cattle: three stots and one mare, twelve oxen, a bull, forty-five cows, three bullocks and six calves. (All this is comparable with 1329-30, apart from a significant increase in dairy cows.) Only one sow was mentioned and no piglets because it was too early in the year. One obvious development compared with previous sets of accounts lies in the number of sheep on the manor: the earl now had a flock of 400, 102 of which had been bought by Thomas at 2s 2d a head. This also reflects a post-Black Death trend: the shift away from arable towards sheep-farming, even on a well-wooded manor like Dorking. Murrain continued to be a problem, requiring constant vigilance. Inspectors of carcases were employed to check any dead animals on the manor and report back to the manor court. In 1365-6, these roles were filled by John Godwyne and Robert at Bourne, who discovered four sheep dead of murrain between December and March, plus another after shearing in August. The sheepskins were sold for 20d, the meat being worthless. Efforts were obviously being made to keep the flock healthy: 8d had been spent on a gallon of vinegar to anoint the earl's sheep.[128] A cow, also dead of murrain, was reported in the final court of the year and, in all cases, the inspectors said that it was nobody's fault, particularly not the shepherd's.

Of course, there were other expenses apart from a pot of sheep-lotion. The Estmell needed repairs, which included the purchase of 100 doornails to mend a broken part of the waterwheel. At the Medmell, two carpenters constructed a new bridge and a new wheel was created by John Stepere, another carpenter. Two millstones were brought from London, at the substantial cost of £10 13s 4d. As previously, they would have been shipped upriver to Kingston and then brought by cart. The ox-shed roof also needed attention: 100 tiles were bought for the purpose, as well as 50 doornails, two wire rings and a hinge.

---

[128] The Latin is unclear but seems to be *vime*, which the author has interpreted as 'vinegar'.

Who Lived on the Manor?

Analysis of the 1365-6 court roll, plus a list of customary tenants owing mill soke in 1370, suggests there were 178 households on the manor, implying a total of 890 residents. However, as before, this is bound to be an underestimate. It may seem surprising that the population should have increased in the twenty-five years since the Black Death but this fits with the national trend. A second wave of pestilence hit the country in 1361-2 and a third in 1369; it was after this that the population of England began to decline and continued to do so throughout the fifteenth century.

Although it's not clear how badly the Black Death affected Dorking, we can get some idea by looking at how many families continue to appear in the manorial records, supplemented by information held in the Poll Tax return of 1381. The Brekesperes and the Bruggesulles were still present on the manor. William Brekespere had a wife called Edith; they seem to have been living at the Bere because William was required to build a new house there and was given a year in which to do it. William also paid pannage for four swine. Richard Brekespere paid pannage for one pig; he also held a customary tenancy, so it seems likely that he had inherited the Brekesperes tenement. If so, his neighbours would have been John Bruggesulle and his wife Margery. John was required to repair his tenement and, as we have seen, got into trouble for assaulting John Hunte. The Broumans were also still living on the manor. Stephen Brouman was an aleseller; he paid pannage for two swine, as did William Brouman. William also paid for three stots to graze on the Homwode. Both were also cited for unspecified defaults and fined 2d. Both held customary tenancies.

If either of the Broumans were living on the family tenement, then their neighbours would have been the Hulles, the Mesbrokes and the Thurbarns. John at Hulle was an aleseller, married to Alice and holding a customary tenancy; another was held by William at Hulle but we don't know who had the family plot. John also paid pannage for two swine and was plaintiff in an unspecified case against John at Horse. Stephen at Mesbroke was headborough of Walde; he also paid pannage for four swine. The Mesbroke customary tenancy was held in 1370 by Agnes, who may be the same woman who appears in the 1381 poll tax return as the wife of Walter at

Mesbroke. Finally, Richard Thurbarn also appears in the court rolls, for an unspecified default and for trespass on the earl's common.

Further south, Gilbert at Hacche was an aleseller who paid pannage for one pig. He held a customary tenancy, as did Margery at Hacche. We don't know what the relationship between them was. The Rushetts don't appear in the 1365-6 court roll but do re-emerge in 1381, when Isabelle, John and Walter at Rushett feature in the court roll. John at Pleystowe was living away from the manor; he paid chevage for the year but also paid pannage for five swine. When he died in November, no heriot was paid to the earl or to the church because he had nothing. His tenement was unclaimed in 1366 but, by 1370, Robert at Pleystowe held it.

The tenancies which housed Pleystowe's immediate neighbours, Clerks, Risbrugges and Taylors, were all occupied. Adam Clerk held the former; he paid pannage for six swine and was one of the affeerers for the manor court, responsible for setting the levels of fines. He also gave an essoin for Thomas at Plesshette. The Taylors tenement was held by Thomas Taylor; one wonders whether he was related to the Matthew and Agnes Taillour who appeared in the View of Frankpledge. (If so, he might not have admitted to it as they were both involved in fights.) William at Risbrugge and Robert at Risbrugge each held a customary tenancy in 1370 but it was Robert who held the family plot: he was required to maintain the King's Highway where it ran beside the property. By 1381, William was married to Felicia and Robert to Joan, with a son called William; in 1365, each of them paid pannage for three swine. At the very edge of the manor, Upbrokes was held by Robert Upbroke. He doesn't appear in the court roll but John Upbroke and his wife do: John was cited for unspecified defaults and there was a scandal regarding their daughter, of which more later. John Wadelshurst probably held the Wadelshurst tenancy but only an Adam Wadelshurst appears in the court roll, victim of an assault by William Moutoun.

On the western side of the manor, the Langshete tenement may have been taken by William, Henry or Adam, all of whom held customary tenancies in 1370. William paid pannage for two swine but the other two don't appear in the court roll, although Henry Langshete, jnr was cited for hiring out his labour in contravention of the assize. As we have seen, the

Bere tenement was held by one of the Brekesperes but the Lythe land was probably held by Maurice at Lythe. He doesn't appear in the court roll but William at Lythe does: he was a carpenter, married to Margery, who also had some arable land and paid pannage for five swine. He appeared as an aleseller and was one of the freeholders who swore fealty in 1365. To the north of the Homwode, John Godwyne, Stephen at Holoweye and Richard Sket all held customary tenancies. John Godwyne was required to repair the building on his property; he paid pannage for two swine and also to graze two mares in the Homwode. He served as inspector of carcases throughout the year 1365-6. Meanwhile, Richard Sket had left the manor without permission but was obviously back by 1370, while Stephen at Holoweye was an aleseller who also paid pannage for two swine.

A couple of surnames associated with customary tenancies had disappeared from the record by this point. One is not unexpected: the Grenehurst tenancy having been alienated in 1344, the name 'de Grenehurst' ceases to appear. The other is 'Sprot'; Sprotstenement was in the hands of John Thurbarn by the early 1380s but we don't know who held it in the 1360s. Among the cottars, even more names had dropped out of the record. However, it must been borne in mind that most of them only appear once, in the Extent. Of those that do appear in other manorial records, Bynorthbroke and Tailleboys had now disappeared (ominously, Henry Bynorthbroke was leasing property in 1347 but not thereafter). However, some cottar families not only survived but seem to have

Broadcasting seed. The crows are back.

prospered. In the 1365-6 court roll, Robert at Bere was described as a common labourer, who paid pannage for two swine. He also leased two crofts containing six acres of villein land to Thomas de Hayton (later priest at Capel) for nine years and another croft of villein land called Blakemanhaugh to Walter Charesmore for seven years. By 1370, he held a customary tenancy, although we don't know which one. William Renger also appears in the 1370 mill soke list as the holder of a customary tenancy. Sixty-five year earlier, his family held a small cotland on the high street, so the Rengers had definitely come up in the world. Two more 'cottar' surnames also continue to appear. John Osweard was an aleseller, who was prosecuted for allowing a cow to trespass in John Kene's oats. He was also accused of keeping a hunting dog without a collar. The other is 'at Hethe'; although we don't know who inherited under Avelina at Hethe's will and nobody of that name appears in the 1365-6 court roll, several at Hethes were living on the manor in the 1380s. These included a William at Hethe who was described as a 'villein of the lord'. This strongly suggests that he was one of Avelina's descendants (and, indeed, that Avelina had been personally unfree).

By the 1360s, all the cotlands seem to have passed into private hands. There was a dispute over the one called Alotyslond. William Noble, heir to the late Nicholas Noble, accused Roger Yonge of holding back three rods of villein land that formed part of the plot; Nicholas had acquired the cotland, holding it by court roll. It's not entirely clear what the problem was but Roger denied it and the homage got into trouble for concealing what went on. Meanwhile, William came to the court and surrendered the Alotyslond into the earl's hand, paying heriot of one horse.

There are hints in the court roll that the earl, in common with other lords, was trying to reassert his rights in the wake of the social upheaval caused by the Black Death, particulary over those who were personally unfree. As mentioned above, Richard Sket was cited in January for leaving the manor without permission; he was fined half a mark but, in March, the whole homage went bail for him, assuring the court that he would be back after Easter. In October, Agnes Peyter was summoned to appear because she had married outside the demesne and without permission. She attended the next court and paid a huge fine of 50s. Given that the fee for controlling her own marriage choices would have been 6s 8d, one wonders what the background was.[129]   More scandalously, there was a case running throughout the year regarding Joan, the daughter of John Upbroke. In November, it was presented that a John Gostrode had an illicit relationship with her (Lat *concubinare*). This was a matter for the manor court because her family was personally unfree, so John Gostrode had committed an offence against the earl. Gostrode was repeatedly summoned to appear at court and, after nearly a year, he paid a fine of one mark. Joan's parents were also required to appear and pay a fine but it's not recorded whether they did.

The small manor of Gostrode lay to the west of the Upbroke half-virgate. In 1326, it was held by a Richard de Gostrode; his lord seems to have been Nicholas de Malemeyns (lord of Ockley manor).[130] No other contemporary information is known about the family but the proximity of the manor to the Upbroke tenement seems significant. Interestingly, in 1384, a John Upbroke paid the 6s 8d fee so that his daughter, Edith, could marry whom he chose. Marriage licences appear very rarely in the Dorking manorial documents, which suggests that the events of 1365-6 continued to reverberate through the Upbroke family.

The case would also have been raised at the Surrey archdeaconry court; unfortunately the records for this period have not survived. However, there does seem to have been a recent visitation by John, archdeacon of Surrey. On 2nd March 1365, John Barbour, the attorney, delivered 8s in silver to Ralph at Heghlond, beadle of Dorking. It seems that the money had been unjustly taken from William at Dene during the visitation and the archdeacon had repaid the money via his summoner, who presumably passed it on to John Barbour. Whether it got back to William is unknown.

As well as trying to assert control over the personally unfree, the earl seems to have attempted to restore his ancient rights to customary labour at a time when resistance against such work was strong.   In March, the

---

[129] The sum of 50s is taken from notes on the court rolls made in the 16thC; assuming the transcription is accurate, it seems excessive.
[130] Brayley (1841), vol V, p.36.

headborough and beadle of Walde were fined because they didn't deliver one man to the reeve to harrow the earl's land 'just as they have been ordered'. In December, the reeve and the whole homage were required to repair the ox-shed against wind and rain and given just under two months to do it, on penalty of half a mark. Although this had always been the responsibility of the customary tenants, the labour had previously been commuted to a money payment: 3½d for gathering withies for the roofs and 2s 5½d for repair of both barn and ox-shed. Finally, as we have seen, a list was drawn up in 1370 naming all the customary tenants who owed mill soke and fining them for not taking their grain to the earl's mill.[131] The fact that all thirty-seven customary tenants were fined suggests concerted action. Perhaps Roger Yonge had continued to levy unjust tolls, as had been asserted in the 1365 View of Frankpledge.

Meanwhile, the property market continued but at a less frantic pace, particularly when compared with the first quarter of the 14thC. John Carpenter had acquired land from Thomas Quarreor, chaplain; he was required to come to court and show the deed, as was John Kentyng for land, previously held by Robert Gylemyn, which he and his wife Joan had acquired from William Smyth. Some years later, John Kentyng and his wife, now named as Isabelle, acquired land from Roger de Freton, clerk (and subsequently dean of Chichester).[132] A deed dated 7th February 1350 shows that Robert at Park granted a messuage and some land to Robert Tepeham. The property lay between land called 'Totefelde' to the north and Maurice de Ewekene's land to the south and extended from 'Brexspersland' on the east to the highway, which makes it easy to pin down on the map.[133] As we have seen, on 13th March 1351, John Chapman, snr gave to Walter Godefray a messuage and curtilage on Holowestret, next to Thomas Fust's tenement. John had inherited it from his father, Peter.[134]

---

[131] See Appendix E.

[132] Pedes Finium, p.147 (24).

[133] SRO K43/57/2. Another deed transferred land and tenements in Ockley from Robert Tepeham to Robert and Matilda at Park, so there seems to have been a swap (SHC K43/58/15).

[134] BL 9038.

There was also some question over the ownership of Oggestoles (a croft containing three acres of land on the eastern edge of the manor) and an acre of free land next to Shamelfeld. They came into the earl's hand because Henry Noble failed to show by what right he came into possession.

More details on property transactions can be found among the 'feet of fines'. John de Saghiere and his wife, Joan, granted two acres in Dorking and Betchworth to Adam Pynkehurst and Adam Geffray of Horsham, plus their respective wives.[135] John at Bere gave a piece of land in Dorking to John Scamaile and his wife, Sibil.[136] John Farman, chaplain, and Walter Chapman, vicar of Dorking, granted a messuage, eight acres of land, three acres of woods and one acre of meadow in Dorking to Robert Sebarn and William Baldwyne and their wives, Margaret and Alice.[137] Several of these names are new to the manorial documents, suggesting that these were investment properties. The Sondes also continued to increase their holdings; a deed from this period shows Edward de la Sonde acquiring land from Walter Godard.[138]

One deed shows how life went on despite the Black Death. In 1379, a series of property transactions between Roger Stub of Dorking and John Whyte of Sutton Scotney, Hampshire, were set out in single document. According to this, on 5th April 1349, Roger had given all his lands and tenements in Dorking to John and his wife Dionysia, who was Roger's sister. On 4th October in the same year, John and Dionysia returned everything to Roger for his lifetime; he had to render any services due to the earl and to pay them a white rose on the feast of St John the Baptist. Thirty years later, the family's circumstances had obviously changed. On 9th June 1379, Roger remitted all the lands to John and Dionysia and, on 11th June, they granted it all to Nicholas Henle and his wife, Agnes. The first two deeds were drawn up before and after the summer when the Black Death was raging but the legal business carried on.[139]

---

[135] Pedes Finium, p.126 (5).
[136] Pedes Finium, p.128 (34).
[137] Pedes Finium, p.139 (68).
[138] BL 9201 & 18663.
[139] BL 9051.

Among those holding freehold property in the second half of the 14thC, at least seventy names can also be seen in pre-Black Death records. A few (Ansty, Bal, Heggere, Henhurst, Horse, Kentyng, Lynne, at Pippe and Yonge) first appeared in Dorking in the 1340s but most are apparent throughout our hundred-year period, from the 1280s to the 1380s. Having said that, a dozen names do disappear after the 1340s, including the Hurlewynes, the Isemongers, the Lovels, the Pages and the de Ewekenes. It's tempting to blame the pestilence for the loss of these families but it's not necessarily the case: women are very hard to trace after they marry and families do die out naturally or move away.

Twenty-two new surnames appeared in the 1360s, fifteen of which continued into the 1380s and beyond. This may well be due to the increased mobility among the population after the Black Death, something which will become even more apparent when we later consider the Poll Tax return.

Archery practice. We don't know where the butts were in Dorking.

How to Make a Living

After the Black Death, the authorities tried to reinstate the status quo regarding wages and customary work. This led to the Statute of Labourers of 1351, a doomed attempt to make ordinary people work for what the lords expected rather than what the market allowed. Luckily for us, the repetitive lists of fines that appear in the 1365 View of Frankpledge provide detailed information on the kind of work being done on Dorking manor.

Some of those fined were common labourers living in Waldeborough who were taking advantage of their ability to hire out their labour for a good price: Robert at Bere, William Bole, John Bruggesulle, Walter Charesmore, William at Churche, Henry Langshete, jnr and Henry at Mounte were all fined 6d. Getting enough labour to bring in the harvest was a particular problem for landlords after the Black Death. Eight Dorking residents were fined for reaping at harvest-time and charging more than was allowed; interestingly, they all lived in Estborough, rather than the more rural part of the manor.[140] Three of them were women.

Seven butchers were cited for breaking the statute: Richard le Haye in Waldeborough, John Donner, Richard Suel and Adam Whytyng in Chippingborough and John Bynnysay, Richard Gylemyn and William at Sonde in Estborough. Bread and fish were also for sale in the town. In Chippingborough, John Kene was the baker and William Inchere and

Reaping the grain at harvest-time. Back-breaking work.

---

[140] They were: Symon Aylward, Thomas Barbour, Dionisia Bongeor, William Coupere, Margary Flecchere, John Kentyng, Matilda at Park and Richard Skynnere.

Henry at Style the fishmongers; in Estborough, there were two bakers (Peter Bonet and Thomas Tournour) and one fishmonger (John A Neve). Chippingborough also housed two tanners, two weavers, three tailors and a cobbler; Estborough a tailor and a weaver.[141] There was a thatcher called Richard Pynchere but it's not specified where he lived. A wheelwright called Thomas at Lompulle and a carpenter called Walter Bakere lived in Foreignborough, reflecting the position of that borough in and around the Homwode.

Thomas Tournour, the baker from Estborough, got into trouble because his wholewheat bread weighed less than it should; he was fined half a mark. He was also described as a 'tenant of Cappilbothe', as were John Carpenter, Stephen Dyghere, John Kene, Juliana Spicer, Richard Tepeham and John Wodeward. The latter all lived in Chippingborough, so what this means is unclear; they were all fined 6d for selling contrary to the statute.

Another aspect of commercial life which the authorities tried to suppress was the practice known as 'forestalling'. A dealer in a particular commodity would go to market first thing and buy supplies which he or she would then sell on. This was seen as unfair: it was expected that everyone should have the opportunity to go and buy at the same price. In Dorking, John de Balne, jnr, John Carpenter, John Kene, John A Neve and John Tanner were all cited as forestalling corndealers. (Clearly, the stock of available Christian names hadn't greatly increased.)

For the first time, we have mention of an inn in Dorking, when Avelina Colvill was described as a victualler and tenant innkeeper. She lived in Estborough, so may have run either of the inns later known as the George and the Cardinal's Hat. The presence of an inn didn't have any discernible impact on the number of alesellers in town, perhaps because the inn catered for people travelling to and from London. 72 people were named in the course of the court year for breaking the assize. Seven were women, three of whom were part of an aleselling family (Agnes Caas, Christiana at Dene

---

141 John Tannere and William Noble; Richard Busche and Gilbert Olyne; Walter Godefray, Matthew Wynneholm and Richard Pyshagh; and Thomas Noble in Chippingborough. John at Medende and William Kymere in Estborough.

and Christiana Deth). The most prolific was Juliana Spicer, who paid the fee eight times. At least four of the men named must have been full-time brewers: Thomas Caas, Stephen Dyghere, Richard Henhurst and William Palmere were subsequently described as such in the 1381 poll tax return. Thomas and Richard were fined six times during the year, Stephen eleven times and William twelve. The aletasters were Adam Whytyng and Walter Godefray, with the latter being replaced by Nicholas Henle in March or April. Most of the amounts paid were the usual 2d or 3d but William Drynkewater was fined 2s because he didn't send for the aletasters. He appeared ten times (out of thirteen reports), so was presumably another of the full-time brewers; if it weren't for the presence of Juliana Drynkewater on the manor, one might wonder whether his surname was a joke or nickname.

An alewife. The alestake above her door shows she has a brew ready.

How to Build a House on a Medieval Manor

In October 1365, three customary tenants were ordered to repair the houses on their tenements. The disrepair of such buildings became more of a problem for landlords after the Black Death, as tenancies were harder to fill. It was the tenants who had to bear the cost of such work, which may account for their reluctance to commit to repairs until threatened with a fine at the manor court. John Bruggesulle and John Godwyne were given until Martinmas (11th November) to do the work, on penalty of 11d each. Neither of them had done so by the November court, so they were given until Candlemas (2nd February) and, at the February court, the whole homage testified that both buildings had been well and suitably repaired. The third tenant ordered to carry out repairs was Walter Peyter, the reeve. He got the work done by December, perhaps because he had been threatened with a penalty of half a mark, being occupied in the earl's service.

Freeholders could also be required to make repairs, as Roger Yonge discovered when he acquired a purpresture (a permitted encroachment on the lord's land) previously held by the late Nicholas Noble. At the July court, Roger was told to rebuild the house on his new land and was given until the Feast of St John the Baptist to do it, on penalty of 40s. He was reminded at the September court but we don't know if he ever completed the work.

Meanwhile, William Brekespere was told to build a new house at the Bere. During the final court of the manorial year, he was given until the following Michaelmas to complete the work, on penalty of 20s. If he intended to do so, he would have had to get started straight away: the process took a year and began in autumn. Houses in Surrey were built on the wealden pattern: timber-framed, with an open hall flanked by two bays jettied at the front. The first job William faced was to sign a contract with the carpenter, who acted as architect and contractor on the whole build. As seen previously, the only carpenter who appeared in the Dorking court roll was Walter Baker, who lived in Foreignborough. (By the time of the Poll Tax return he was described as a holder of land, so he obviously went up in the world). Additionally, two carpenters named in 1381 were living in the manor in 1365-6: Thomas at Lompulle (who was then described as a wheelwright) and William Lythiere (who appeared as an aleseller).

As there was no right for tenants on Dorking manor to take timber for building, William would have had to buy the wood he needed from the earl. Given that the total cost of building a house has been estimated at £30, with a third being payable up front at Christmas for timber, this might seem far beyond what a customary tenant could afford. Perhaps William borrowed the money. (The risk of getting into debt may also, of course, account for the reluctance of tenants to embark on such building projects.) The primary timber required was oak, to build the frame and the beam which acted as a foundation, supported on stones to prevent it rotting from below. Cut at about 25 years old, oak was perfect for such construction because it was straight-growing and increased in strength from the moment it was cut. After the timber had been sawn into baulks, the frame would have been created at the carpenter's yard, put together with mortice and tenon joints held by pegs. Once assembled, the whole thing would have been marked up and dismantled, to be transported to the site of the building. Other types of wood were also needed. Elm was used for boards to make doors and

An artist's impression of a newly built, timber-framed house.

shutters, ash for roofing spars and chestnut for lathes on which daub was plastered. The schedule consisted of two weeks for felling the trees, three months for hewing, another three months for making the frame and at least two weeks to erect the structure. The carpenter's role should have been completed by midsummer, when a fire could be lit and kept going to dry everything out. [142]

That wasn't the end of the job, of course. The roof would have been tiled, probably using a locally-made product. There is a record in 1354 of 550 plain tiles being sent to Esher from Dorking, while the manorial accounts for 1376 show 100 tiles being bought for 6d to repair the ox-shed roof.[143] Unfortunately, it's not specified from whom. A Walter Tyghelere appears once in the court roll, as plaintiff in a plea of debt, so perhaps it was he who supervised the creation of William's new roof. As well as tiles, a large quantity of nails would have to be bought, along with hinges for doors. The Isemonger family had disappeared from the record by this point, so we don't know who was providing such iron objects in Dorking. Once the roof was up, the walls would be made out of wattle hurdles interlaced with lathes. Daub (a mixture of clay or sand and dung) was applied to the lathes and, once dry, limewashed. The downstairs floor would probably have consisted of crushed chalk, hardened off with sour milk (or urine).[144]

Unfortunately, no contract or set of personal accounts survive to tell us how much a house built on the manor of Dorking might have cost. However, a deed dated 27th October 1379 possibly includes an example of speculative building in the town. In this document, John Chapman (vicar of Godalmyng), William Peyto (rector of Buckland) and Ralph at Heghlond granted to William Godynge a tenement called 'Nywehalle'. The property

---

[142] Information on construction is derived from a talk given to the Newdigate Local History Society on 2nd March 2020 by Stephen Gray, entitled 'Building a Medieval House'.

[143] Accounts for the Manor of Esher in the Winchester Pipe Rolls, p.368.

[144] Such buildings were sturdy constructions and some have survived to this day. The Domestic Buildings Research Group has surveyed many houses in Capel and, according to their website (dbrg.org.uk), Highland Cottage dates from the early 14thC, the west wing of Taylors Farm from c.1345, Ketleas from c.1389 and the barn at Pleystowe farm from c.1400.

lay between that of Richard at Sonde and of Henry at Sonde. Its position in Dorking town is unspecified but it seems likely that it later became part of the substantial Sonde property holding.[145]

A boy stealing cherries from a tree.

The Church

Two aspects of popular engagement in the later medieval church can be seen in Dorking at this time: devotion to the Blessed Virgin Mary and reliance on intercessory masses to help the souls of the departed through purgatory. The doctrine of purgatory, as precisely defined in the late 12[th]C, specified that between heaven and hell lay an intermediate stage, where the souls of the dead might purge their sins. Their sufferings could be alleviated by the celebration of masses. The wealthy endowed chantry chapels, where mass-priests sang a continual round of prayers for the souls of the benefactor and their loved ones. The less well-to-do could join a confraternity (or brotherhood) for the same purpose.

There is no evidence for a chantry chapel in Dorking church but there was a brotherhood, which had an altar dedicated to the Blessed Virgin Mary, served by one priest. The brotherhood was open to both men and women and, by the time of its suppression in 1548, it had been given eleven parcels of land, including one next to the Cardinal's Hat, another little garden in Hamstede and various properties on Suthestret and Eststret.[146] The rest lay further outside the town. One of the plots comprised a house and garden, which was probably where the brothers and sisters held their annual feast; others would have provided income. The priest was primarily engaged in singing masses for the souls of the brotherhood's departed members but he would also have assisted the vicar, especially in singing the Office and the Mass. The brotherhood probably led the annual procession at Candlemas, when every parishioner brought a candle to church to celebrate the churching of the Blessed Virgin Mary.

By the mid-14[th]C, the church building had undergone some improvements. The nave had been heightened by the addition of a clerestory and widened by the construction of two side aisles. A large and decorative five-light window was created at the chancel end, in the curvilinear style; another window of similar size was also created at the west end. This was in the perpendicular style, so could have been built during the late 14[th]C or, more probably, the 15[th]C. It seems likely that the

---

[146] CPR EdVI, vol III, p.108.

windows in the tower were also widened at this stage. The improvements to the chancel would have been paid for by the rector and those to the nave by Dorking's parishioners. Donations were voluntary but wouldn't have been difficult to collect: enthusiasm for beautifying one's parish church was widespread in the 14th and 15th centuries. It was the parishioners who paid for the principal image of the saint to whom their church was dedicated. In Dorking, this was St Martin, who is usually depicted on horseback, sharing his cloak with a beggar. At the chapel in Ewekene, it was St Lawrence, who is traditionally shown being martyred on a griddle. The congregation were also expected to supply the processional cross and everything necessary for services: the priest's vestments, plus the chalice, missal, candles and books, particularly those with musical notation.

The nave and chancel would have been separated by a rood screen, depicting the figure of the crucified Christ flanked by those of the Blessed Virgin Mary and St John. At the time of the dissolution, Dorking church had 42 brass candlesticks and two standard ones for the high altar. Many of the former were probably used to light the rood loft.[147] Other than that, we have no information about the interior of Dorking's medieval church, although contemporary examples suggest that the walls of the nave would have been highly decorated and the glass in the new windows painted. The floor, uncluttered by benches or pews, was strewn with rushes. At the west end, one would find the font, made of stone and kept locked. Information about the interior of the chapel at Ewekene is similarly scanty, althouth it may be at about this time that buttresses were added to its thick stone walls.[148]

We don't know the names of any of the early brotherhood priests. Nor do we know the name of the chaplain of Capel at this point. One possible candidate for the latter is mentioned in the court roll, when John Carpenter showed a deed through which he acquired the land of Thomas Quareor,

---

[147] Lewis André (1899), p.6. The will of Richard Coter in 1486 refers to three lights at Dorking church and includes the earliest reference to the dedication to St Martin (Surrey Wills, p.42 (142)).
[148] Malden (1930), p.173.

chaplain. Thomas was from Dorking and had been appointed as an acolyte in 1353 but we know no more about him.[149]

The vicar of Dorking in 1365 was Walter Chapman. He appeared twice in the court roll: he brought a plea of debt against John de Balne, jnr and was accused of killing a hare in the earl's demesne, which he denied. Walter was also involved in an enquiry into the advowson of Abinger church. The advowson was split between the lords of Abinger manor and the nearby Paddington manor; when John Kyngesfolde acquired the lordship of Paddington, he presented a priest called Robert Snokeshull as vicar. It seems that the lord of Abinger, Thomas Jerconville, objected because an enquiry was held by Walter, vicar of Dorking, and John, vicar of Send. The result was that the advowson was united and Thomas Jerconville presented Robert Snokeshull to the living: the perfect compromise.[150] Interestingly, two of the people involved are known to us. John Kyngesfolde was one of the nineteen men to whom Earl Richard enfeoffed

An artist's impression of Dorking church from the southeast, showing the new east window.

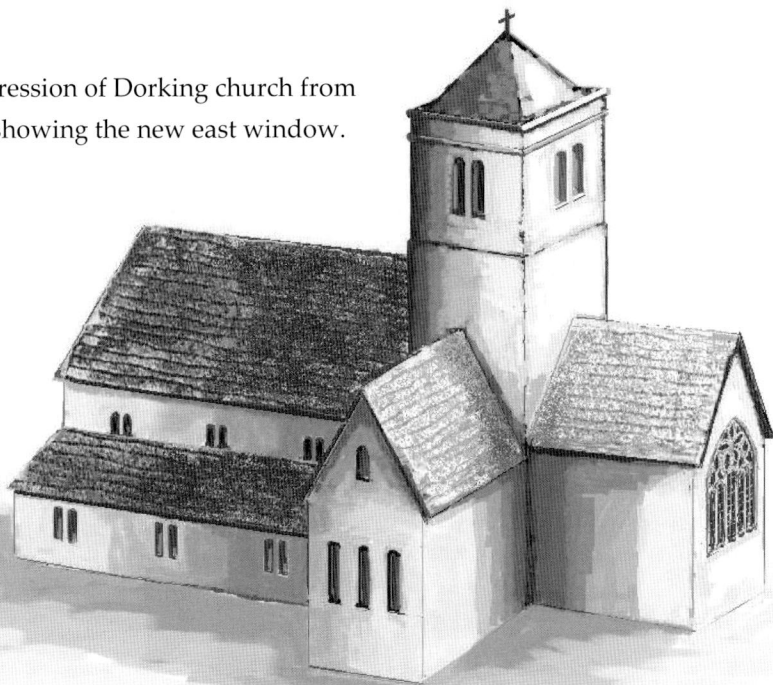

[149] Edington register, pt 2, p.168 (839 & 840).
[150] Edington register, pt 1, pp.235-6 (1636 & 1637).

his land in Surrey, Sussex and Wales; he probably also held the Grenehurst tenement at this point and later served as the earl's steward. Robert Snokeshull was one of the freeholders who swore fealty in 1365.

Walter was succeeded as vicar by Roger de Brecham, who served until his death in 1378. He was followed by John Appletone.[151]

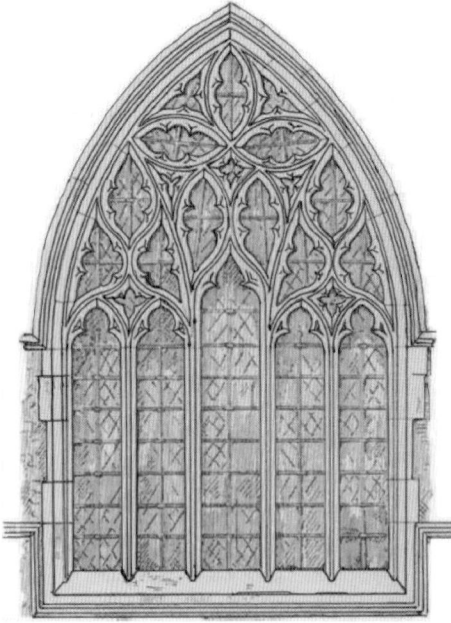

The east window, in the curvilinear style.

The west window, in the later perpendicular style.

---

[151] Edington register, pt 2, p.50 (385) & Wykeham register, vol I, p.99 (94).

Richard, Earl of Arundel and Surrey, inherited the manor of Dorking because his mother, Alice, was sister of the late earl, John. His father had been executed when Mortimer and Queen Isabelle held power: Earl Richard only gained full restitution of his paternal lands and honours in 1354, by Act of Parliament. Always loyal to Edward III, he fought several times in France and was one of the principal commanders at the Battle of Creçy in 1346. While underage, he had been married to Isabelle le Despenser, daughter of the Earl of Gloucester; despite having several children, the marriage was annulled on grounds of coercion and the earl then married Eleanor, daughter of the Earl of Lancaster. They had six children and, when the earl died on 24 January 1375/6, his eldest son, Richard, inherited Dorking manor (among much else).

It has been said that, at his death, Earl Richard was the wealthiest man in England.[152] This wealth had not been inherited: although he had regained his father's land, most of the moveable property had not been recovered. Throughout his life, the earl amassed a fortune drawn from the income of his many estates, enterprising landlordship (especially regarding sheep farming), investment of his capital with merchants and financiers, favours granted in return for credit and the profits of his influence at court.[153] His son must have inherited well over 80,000 marks in cash and outstanding debts.[154]

Tracing Dorking men in the London records is more difficult by this stage, due to the preponderance of true surnames (rather than the descriptive 'of Dorking'). One man who was trading in the City was the Walter Skamaill who was involved in two assaults in Dorking. In 1362, he owed money to John de Stody, vintner and alderman of Vintry Ward, along with John de Nottingham and John Skamayll. Nearly twenty years later, Walter owed 100s to John Sewale, a citizen and stockfishmonger, so it's not clear what business he was in.[155] There may have been another

---

[152] Given-Wilson (1991), p.1.
[153] Ibid, p. 21.
[154] Ibid, pp.14-15.
[155] PRO C241/145/124 & C241/175/47.

contemporary connection between Dorking and the Vintry. One vintner who was very active in this period was called Gilbert Bonet; perhaps he was related to the Bonets on Dorking manor.

The effigies of Earl Richard and Countess Eleanor, depicted as if they were created in brass. The originals are in stone and can now be found at Chichester cathedral.

The Year of the Poll Tax and the Peasants' Revolt: 1381

Mondays and Thursdays were market-days in Dorking. The town would have been busy with shoppers as the townsfolk were joined by those who lived south of the Homwode and villagers from nearby Betchworth or Brockham. Boards were let down in front of the buildings around the marketplace and temporary stalls appeared for the day. During 1381, Roger Yonge was in charge, receiving tolls from those selling goods or livestock and making sure things ran smoothly. He had paid £16 to 'farm' both the market and the mills. As the latter were worth slightly less than the former, it seems likely that the market was expected to bring in a profit of about £10 for the year. It has been suggested that any market where more than £10 a year was received in tolls would have seen hundreds of people doing business there in any given week.[156] Even though revenue in 1381-2 was obviously expected to be less than in 1329-30 (when £20 was paid for the farm of market and mills), it seems that Dorking market was still going strong.

Many markets in England were licensed by charter from the king but that wasn't the case for Dorking. The market was already up and running in 1278, when the liberties of the Earl de Warenne were assessed. The fact that it was held twice a week shows that the demand was there, which wasn't always the case with a chartered market: many lords requested charters for new markets in the 12th and 13th centuries but they didn't always thrive. Of course, markets weren't just for shopping. They were places where news could be exchanged, where official proclamations were made and punishments meted out. In the summer of 1381, one of the subjects of conversation must have been Wat Tyler's rebellion, of which more later.

---

[156] Masschaele (2002), p.387. His calculations are based on tolls such as a halfpenny for the sale of a horse or a farthing for a load of grain.

At the Manor Court

For the first time, we may be able to name one of the clerks whose painstaking and repetitive work allows us to catch a glimpse of life on the manor. The accounts for 1381-2 name a John Pebelowe as the earl's clerk; he appeared in the document because he received a payment from William at Mounte, the wodeward. Other entries record 5s being spent on parchment for the court rolls in the 'Surrey division' and 3d for a small sack in which to carry the rolls.

There are some hints that the Dorking court wasn't running all that smoothly. Walter at Mesbroke evidentaly wasn't told that he had been elected as beadle of Walde: he was replaced in January by Richard Sket and the whole homage was fined for handling the election badly. At the beginning of November, Walter Charesmore, one of the Walde aletasters, was cited for not attending court to present his findings, while the Dorking aletasters (John Carpenter and John at Honchones) were fined for the same in December. The following month, both Walter and William Brekespere, the other Walde aletaster, failed to attend.

There also seems to have been some resistance to contributing to the common fine. In Chippingborough, John at Dawe, snr and Walter Kene were fined during the 1381 View of Frankpledge for not paying.[157] Later in the same court year, Robert Kene and Richard Spicer were described as 'rebellious' for not paying; Robert was subsequently fined but Richard questioned the accusation, saying that his payment had been made. The following year's View of Frankpledge reveals three more cases: Henry at Sonde and Hugh at Sonde in Chippingborough and John at Chert in Foreignborough also rebelled against their headboroughs. Perhaps, in light

A clerk taking dictation.

---

[157] They were described as *non sunt insocabit*, which seems to mean they were ignoring the social ties to their headborough and tithing.

of contemporary political events, the payment of a fixed common fine every year regardless of how many men were in each tithing had become more burdensome.

The 1381 View of Frankpledge included several matters that seem to have been previously overlooked and then picked up by a special jury.[158] These twelve men reported three acts of violence in Foreignborough which the headborough and tithing had concealed: John at Dene had assaulted Richard Balcome, Roger Pypyn had assaulted John Brokere and John Bal of Anstey had assaulted Henry Charesmore and drawn blood. In Waldeborough, the road next to John Syre's property was reported as defective; again the headborough and tithing had concealed the problem. The jury also reported that John Carpenter, jnr and Henry Olyne were 'common nightwalkers' who disturbed the peace in Chippingborough. Being out after dark contravened the Statute of Winton; their pledges included John Carpenter and Gilbert Olyne, who were presumably their fathers. John Carpenter, jnr was also fined for entering the house of Joan Frowe at night; again, his behaviour had been concealed, this time by the headborough and tithing of Estborough. It's not clear how these nightwalkers were caught, as both the urban tithings admitted not keeping the vigil according to the Statute of Winton, which meant a 6d fine for Estborough and 12d for Chippingborough. The fact that a jury had been brought together to investigate such matters rather suggests that the usual reporting structures were failing somewhat. Also at the December court, it came to light that William Upbroke had occupied John Godwyne's tenement without permission for ten years. He was fined, as was the whole homage for concealing it.

One very striking aspect of the court roll for 1381-2 is the large number of pleas of debt being pursued through the court. 65 plaintiffs brought cases against 73 defendants; this compares with ten cases in 1282-3 and twelve in 1365-6. The high number continued the following year, so it wasn't an aberration, but it's difficult to know how to interpret it. Were more people

---

[158] The jurymen were: Robert Ashcombe, William Bialde, Thomas Bonet, John Carpenter, John at Chert, Robert Clerk, Nicholas Henle, Adam at Homwode, John Ode, Henry at Sonde, Hugh at Sonde and John Wadelshurst.

getting into debt because they were struggling or is this a sign of increased commercial activity? Alternatively, it could reflect a change in recording methods or an increase in people using the manor court for this purpose. Moneylending had always been part of manorial life; cash was in short supply, so informal lending arrangements were made between neighbours who had surplus coin and those who didn't, with the market being a popular place to arrange loans. It seems that interest was charged at around 10% but, since usury was both sinful and illegal, it was disguised. A number of cases in the Dorking court roll refer to 'damages' as well as the principal sum owed, which might demonstrate disguised interest. Although women could both borrow and lend, we see little of this in Dorking: Matilda Bal was the only female plaintiff listed in 1381-2 and, of four female defendants, only Elizabeth at Sonde was named alone. The other three were all joint defendants with their husbands.

We have background information about several of those who appear as plaintiffs: twenty were holders of land, fourteen tradesmen, three labourers or smallholders, three were described as being in service and one was the chaplain at Capel. Among the defendants, a similar pattern can be seen, apart from in one group: eleven labourers or smallholders borrowed money. These are precisely the people that would have limited access to cash during most of the year, so it's not surprising that they were more likely to be borrowers or to owe money. In only three of these debt cases are we provided with any additional detail. William Stilere was obviously working as a carter: he had carried charcoal to Kingston for Walter Charesmore but not been paid his 12s fee. He also sued Roger Langshete for 5s for carrying charcoal to Leatherhead. Stephen Dighere also brought a case, via his attorney, against William at Hambreche for 6d which he had entrusted to him and a cartload of wood worth 10d, which William had kept for four years. William admitted the debt and paid the 6d, plus a 2d fine, but said the wood had been intended to be shared between them.

In contrast, only twenty-three cases of trespass came up in 1381-2. John at Chert was cited by the reeve for breaking into the lord's pinfold with his beasts, alongside John Coker, William at Dene and Laurence Ingelby, while Walter Bradebrugge was distrained to answer regarding his boar which had got onto the earl's land. He was ultimately fined 6d. A number of residents, named throughout this year and the next as 'John Tannere, Alice Kene and others' were repeatedly summoned to answer regarding pannage in the Homwode and the Innome; evidently, they had been letting their swine roam during the restricted period. In December, John Tannere was also cited for driving a cow into the Homwode outside the correct time and Alice Kene for the same with a horse. They weren't the only ones: Adam at Homwode had done the same with two horses, William Hasebroke with one horse, Walter Bakere with two cows, Thomas at Lompulle with three bullocks, Hugh Netelfolde with two bullocks, John Netelfolde with twelve bullocks and Thomas at Sandhulle with two bullocks. Fines were 2d for a horse and 1d for cattle.

Poaching also gave the earl's men trouble. John at Chert and Richard Balcome were fined for taking rabbits, Richard with a ferret which was confiscated by the warrener. John at Chambre of Chichester, Ralph at Heghlond and John Carpenter, jnr were also prosecuted for hunting rabbits in the earl's warren. This was a particularly current issue: in 1390, a law was passed which ordained that 'no manner of artificer, labourer or any other layman, which hath not lands or a tenement to the value of 40s a year ... shall have or keep from henceforth any greyhound or other dog to hunt; nor shall they use ferrets, nets, snare nor cords nor other engines for to take or destroy deer, hares, nor conies, nor other gentlemen's game, upon pain of one year's imprisonment.'[159] However, for John at Chert, the matter may have signified something deeper. In December 1384, he came to court and admitted to hunting on his own land below the earl's warren, advocating in full court that he could and ought to be able to hunt his own land as he wished. The following April, a jury presented that he had been seized and taken to Reigate castle, having refused to justify himself on penalty of 100s. We don't know what happened but John was probably right in his assertion: the Placita de Quo Warranto, which set out the liberties of the Earl de Warenne, states that the earl had warren in all his land of Dorking and Betchworth but didn't have it in the land of his free men of the same manor.

---

[159] Statutes of the Realm (1816), vol II, p.65.

Trouble and Strife

Various cases of violence between residents were recorded through the usual channels during the View of Frankpledge. Most of the trouble took place in town. In Estborough, Richard Smyth and Thomas Robes had a fight; both were cited for assaulting the other. Thomas also drew blood from John Bonet. Other fights occurred between John Soutere and Margery Lythiere and between Roger Pypyn and John Luwyns and John Carpenter, jnr, when Roger drew blood from John Luwyns. Alice Bonet was also cited for assaulting Alice Oslake. Chippingborough was even more rowdy: Hugh at Sonde assaulted Walter Tigelere and Robert Kene assaulted John Shaldeforde and John Otteforde, drawing blood. There was also further trouble between women: Matilda Suel assaulted Catrin Frye and Elizabeth Sonde assaulted Felicia Suel. In all these cases, the victims successfully raised the hue and cry against their assailants; however, Matilda Bourere unjustly raised it against John at Honchones and was fined. In Foreignborough, John Noble assaulted Agnes Bachelere and, as we have seen, several cases went unreported by the tithing. There was no such trouble reported in Walde: as usual, this tithing was more concerned with roads being impassable. The ditches alongside the King's Highway at Hilemed, Hokeland, Knolleland and Southale needed to be scoured by Walter Peyter, Richard Sket, Robert Clerk and Adam at Homwode, respectively. Robert Clerk was also responsible for repairing the highway at Smythe.

In April, John Carpenter, snr was reported for slandering John at Honchones, his fellow aletaster and sometime affeerer of the court. He might have been punished using the new cucking-stool made that year out of the earl's timber. This object, which had been referred to in the 1329-30 accounts as a 'trebuchetto', was now called a 'shelfyngstool'. Its purpose was the same: to parade the wrongdoer around the town and shame him or her.

The Demesne

The manorial officials in 1381-2 were William Upbroke, reeve, Nicholas Henle, beadle of Dorking, and Richard Sket, beadle of Walde. All three men had previously been and would continue to be involved in the running of the manor. William Upbroke held a virgate of land. He was personally unfree and also held at least one other tenement; unfortunately, we don't know anything about his family. Richard Sket was also personally unfree. He held half a virgate and was married to Matilda, while Nicholas Henle was an attorney who lived in Foreignborough with his wife, Agnes. Presumably his role as beadle stemmed from property he held in villeinage.[160]

Receipts for the manor were £140 12s 3¼d, with £42 8s 10d carried over from the previous year when Adam Clerk had been reeve. Expenses totalled £108 7s 4½d. Superficially, William's accounts are very similar to those drawn up by Walter at Hulle, fifty years previously. However, there had been some developments. Increased or new rents for a number of tenements are listed at length, including 3s new rent payable by Nicholas Henle for the croft called Oggestoles and an acre of land at Shamelfeld. These new or increased rents brought in just under 17s on top of the usual fixed rents received from the customary tenancies. Not all the property at the earl's disposal was let: the accounts refer to a dozen unleased properties or pieces of land, including the Bertone and a croft called Ankershagh.[161] Most of these remained 'in the lord's hand' at the end of the accounting year, although some tenements and messuages which had formerly been held by Roger Jerconville were eventually leased to William Palmere, the warrener. The cotlands known as Ringereslond and Claricie Sweteriche's were demised at farm to John Honchones and John Tannere, respectively. Strangely, the Tolhous was listed in the accounts as untenanted, despite Roger Yonge presumably using it as a base from which to run the market.

---

[160] The 1381-2 accounts are damaged just at this point, so we don't know the size of Nicholas Henle's customary tenancy.

[161] Ankershagh may be where the anchoress (female recluse) of Dorking had lived in seclusion during the 1240s, in which case it was probably near the church. See CLR, p.488.

The earl was owed nearly the same amount of fixed rent as in 1329-30 and received exactly the same payments in lieu of hens and eggs, gilt spurs and cumin. Tallage and the common fine were also paid at the same fixed rate but receipts from pannage and from the manor court were rather low. Pannage and the driving of other beasts into the Homwode brought in 16s 1d (compared with £2 6s 9d in 1329-30) and the court perks totalled £3 15s 4d (compared with £9 5s 10d). Does this reflect a drop in population or in participation? If those working the land were turning to other ways to make a living, it might be the latter.

There had obviously been some changes in the way the demesne was being run. For a start, the earl's servants were more involved than before. William recorded 5s paid to three virgaters and fourteen ferlingsmen for harrowing but 2s 1d was then deducted from his calculations as some of the work had been done by the earl's harrower. Servants from the earl's household assisted with weeding, mowing and binding hay, so the tenants were only paid 9s 10d for this work, less than in 1329-30. 3s 4d was paid for two furlongs of new fencing around the Lese but only 18d for one furlong at the Innome because the earl's servants helped. Another example of change lies in the management of the dairy herd, which was now being carried out at arms-length, with cows and calves being leased for a fixed sum per year. In this way, £6 8s was received by the earl from 32 cows and calves. This wasn't the first year this had happened: both the previous year's beadles had to account for money received for the farm of 22 cows and five cows respectively.

Other aspects of farming the earl's demesne continued as before. The customary tenants paid the same sums in lieu of their labour. Roughly the same number were paid to do the work, including 26s 2d for reaping and binding barley, oats and vetch. However, getting people to do this work was evidently becoming more difficult: in the following year, Joan at Bere, Aldith at Clerhole, John at Hulle, William at Hulle, William Langshete, Robert at Risbrugge, William at Risbrugge, Joan Taillour and John Upbroke were each fined 6d for ignoring a summons to reap at Lammas. Presumably this was connected with the general rise in wages: at the 1381 View of Frankpledge, ten people were fined for charging excessive rates for collecting grain at harvest. All bar one were women and all lived in the town.[162]

Grain and woodland products were still being handled directly by the reeve and the wodeward: £5 1s 5d was received from sales of barley, oats and vetch, while £1 3s 4d was taken for fourteen loads of charcoal made at the Innome, at 20d per load. There were no sales of underwood that year and almost no grazing rights were sold, primarily because it was used for the earl's beasts. (8s of pasture in the Brokwick was leased to William at Mounte but that was all.) The earl's flock was still substantial. 300 wethers were washed and sheared, at a rate of 10d per 100, with the work done as piece-work. Murrain continued to be a problem: eleven sheepskins from animals which had died of the disease were sold for 3d each and six gallons of butter and three gallons of tar were bought for sheep-salve, at 8d a gallon. Murrain also killed a mare, an ox and a cow. 25 sheep were sold after shearing for £1 17s 6d and 14 piglets were sold for 9s 4d because they could not be maintained on the manor.

The earl's harrower received 4s per annum. Other stipends were paid to the Master of the Household (6s per year) and various unspecified servants (5s 6d). No mention is made of wages for the ploughmen but there

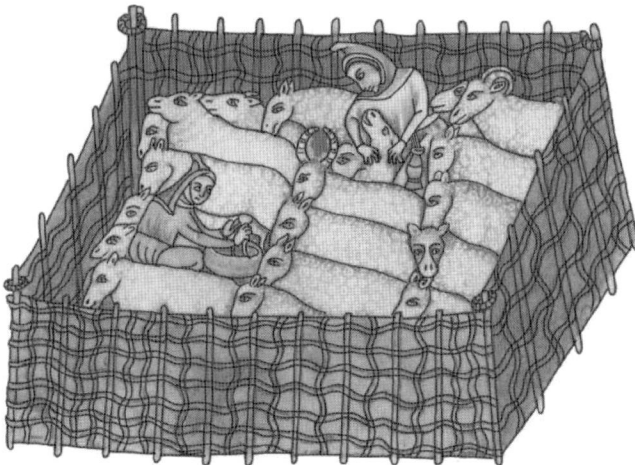

A sheepfold. Note the ointment being applied.

[162] They were: Matilda Bemond, Juliana Carpenter and Margery Skynnere in Estborough; Joan Noble, Richard Spicer, Joan his wife, Marona Sporiere, Felicia Suel, Matilda Suel and Agnes Wychefs in Chippingborough.

were plough expenses: the smith was paid 6s 8d for tipping a plough with steel, while iron supports and a share-beam was bought for 3d. Another plough was made new at a cost of 6d (presumably by the carpenter). The harrow also needed ironwork to replace 40 teeth, while eight oxen and five other cattle were shod in iron.

Mill expenses that year were £9 9s 8d. Most of the work was needed at the Medmell, although the Estmell also required a new spindle and two trendle-wheels. Much of the expense at the Medmell stemmed from transporting timber to the mill and the £5 paid to Robert Shete, the carpenter, for the required work. Henry Oslak was also involved: he was paid £3 13s 7d for work on the mill-pond. Such heavy expenditure had to be authorised by both the constable at Reigate, John Broun, and the earl's receiver, Sir William Peytow. At least the situation wasn't as bad as the previous year, when four carpenters had to be employed to make new the floodgates which had been broken by a great flood of water.

Another expense in 1381-2 stemmed from improvements to the steward's chamber. A tiler and his boy were hired to re-roof it and John Masoun was employed to make a fireplace with a reredos (a strengthening wall of tiles at the back), the whole job priced at 2s. The work on the roof required 2,000 tiles, a quarter of lime, 100 doornails for mending the 'dudposts' and 100 hacknails; perhaps some of the tiles were used to create the reredos. At least work on the barn and ox-shed was comparitively light: only 2s 5d was spent on repairs to the barn roof by the customary tenants, while the aforementioned tiler also made fast the ox-shed. Cart expenses came in at 6s, being 2s 6d for one pair of wheels made from the earl's timber and one pair of metal plates bought for 12d. Axle grease cost 4d for the year and a new wood-carrying waggon was bought for 20d.

There was obviously some work going on at Arundel castle. Five cartloads of Baltic timber bought in London were unloaded en route, with 12d paid in expenses to the men who brought them. The structure at the castle now known as the Bevis Tower was described as 'new built' in Earl Richard's will; perhaps this large-scale timber was for the roof.[163]

---

[163] See The Castle Studies Group Journal No.19 2005-6, pp.9-21.

Another of the earl's employees was the warrener, William Palmere. He was paid a penny a day (£1 10s 4d for 1381-2). Out of a total of 633 rabbits on the warren, he sold 120 to John Clerk, poulterer of London, for 3½d each. He also supplied 28 rabbits as gifts: 24 to the Countess of Hereford and four to the Bishop of Ely. Unfortunately, three acres of oats couldn't be harvested because of destruction by the earl's rabbits; we don't know if William got into any trouble about it. William was probably living at the lodge, which by this time may not have been a comfortable experience: five years later, the building was pulled down and completely rebuilt, due to rotten timbers. The carpenter was paid £2 2s 4d for 127 days' work and the new building required 2,000 stone-nails, 500 flat-nails, 400 plank-nails and 440 'middel'-nails for the structure and the roof. The latter was of Horsham stone, supplied from the store at Reigate castle, and the tiler was paid 11s. Lime and ridge-pieces for the roof cost 5s 4d and 8d, respectively. Plenty of timber must have been supplied from the earl's woods as two sawyers were paid 3s 4d to saw timber for five days. Finally, wattling, daubing and pegging cost 10s. In all, the rebuild came in at a penny shy of £4. If the structure followed the pattern of other lodges from the period, then the result would be a two-storey building, the upper floor providing accommodation for the warrener and the lower used for the secure storage of carcases and pelts; two hooks and hinges plus a lock and a

An artist's impression of the warrener's lodge.

131

key were bought the following year. Other examples of such lodges have fireplaces but no mention of such is made in the 1386-7 accounts; given that a fireplace had only just been installed in the steward's chamber, perhaps this is unlikely. It seems that all the rabbits in the warren were sold that year, presumably to cover the cost: 476 rabbits went for £5 19s.

William Palmere appeared several times as an aleseller in the court roll for 1381-2 and was described as a brewer in the poll tax return. He and his wife, Beatrix, also came to the manor court to show the deed by which they acquired a piece of land from William at Hoke and his wife, Isabelle. Twice in the court roll, William Palmere 'warrener in the same place' features in his official capacity; assuming that this is the same man, one wonders whether Beatrix lived with him in the warrener's lodge or whether his role was more part-time than appears in the accounts.

Although the accounts give no hint of any friction between those running the manor, the court roll tells a different story. Arrears from 1380-1 included 22s due from Richard Sket, alongside sums from Adam Clerk, the reeve, John Wadelshurst, beadle of Dorking, and William at Mounte, the wodeward. The latter three are recorded as paying the money to the earl's receiver but Richard Sket's name is not on the list.

There seems to have been bad blood between Richard Sket and Adam Clerk. At the end of the court held on the 28th January 1381/2, Richard disparaged and spoke badly of Adam, saying that Adam was false and that he should have been hanged seven years past. Richard was fined 40d for contempt of the earl and his court. This seems to relate to an accusation (recorded in the court roll for June 1382) that Adam unjustly withheld 22d which he owed to Richard, Richard having paid it for him to the earl's father for oats. Richard claimed 6d damages but Adam denied the accusation and waged his law. The next court roll doesn't survive but, by 1384-5, the matter seems to have been settled.

Previously, at the court held on 4th November, Richard had sued Adam for debt, asserting that he had unjustly detained Richard's part of the money received after the death of the previous earl, owed at Easter 1379. He also sued for 2s rent of the Osbarneslond tenement, which he said was also owed since Michaelmas in the same year. Adam denied both charges. Adam subsequently sued Richard for 18s which he said was owed since Christmas 1380 for four cows which had been leased. Richard denied it but abandoned his suit.

As well as the feud with Adam Clerk, Richard was in other sorts of trouble. On 25th November, everyone at court told the steward that he had leased a tenement to John at Pleystowe and William Gauge without permission and that the homage had concealed it. He was also bailed to satisfy the earl by the day after Easter regarding ten cows that had been demised at farm for 11s per head; ten people said in court that they had paid the money.[164] Adam Clerk also accused Richard of unjustly detaining 3s he had received from Richard Tepeham, which should have been paid to Adam as the reeve. Richard denied it but a levy was subsequently put on his goods and chattels in order to recover the money. William Gauge was summoned several times and, in April, it came to light that Richard had leased him 40 acres of villein land for seven years, without permission. In 1382-3, Richard leased five crofts of land to William, this time with the earl's approval.

Richard was an interesting character. The 1365-6 court roll refers to his leaving the manor without permission on two occasions. The first time, the homage went bail that he would return to receive the villein land which he had been offered but, the second time, the homage was penalised for not producing him regarding a plea of trespass. He didn't appear in the pannage list, so it seems that he was a young man with other plans than tamely taking over his family plot. In contrast, Adam Clerk was one of the affeerers during the same court year, perhaps already set on a course of official service. Adam didn't serve as reeve again after 1380-1, although he was affeerer in 1384-5 and served on a jury. Richard was re-elected as beadle in 1384, -5 and -6 and was reeve by 1391.

In the Extent, William le Sket was described as holding half a furlong of land. There are two properties labelled 'Sket' on the map, both adjoining Cotmandene. Perhaps the smaller was the original plot and the larger the

---

[164] They were: William Brekespere, John at Helle, William at Hille, Margery Langshete, John at Pleystowe, Richard Risbrugge, William at Risbrugge, William at Roggers, John Upbroke and John Wadeleshurst.

half-virgate that Richard held in 1381. Richard had other property interests: in the same year, he was asked to show how he had entered the lord's land called Sywardislond and for what service he held it. The property is part of the Ewekene but Richard obviously didn't hang on to it, as it was let the following year to Robert at Chert. Richard must also have held the Hokeland, as he was reported to the View of Frankpledge as being responsible for repairing the King's Highway next to the property. By the time of his death in 1403, he held the properties known as Gages, Rugges and le Hylde.[165]

Bees buzzing around a skep.

---

[165] Day & Ettlinger (2015), p.11.

Who Lived on the Manor?

As well as townspeople, manorial residents and villagers, Dorking on market-day would have been visited by servants doing the shopping for their master or mistress. The court roll for 1382-3 names three of them: John (householder of William Caas), Isabelle (householder of Hugh at Sonde) and Thomas (householder of Adam Whytyng). However, it is the 1381 poll tax return which provides the first real indication of the presence of those in service on the manor, naming thirty-two such people. Two Latin terms are used: *serviens* and *servient*. The former means 'serving' or 'subservient to'; the latter can be translated as 'servant' or as 'labourer'.

Everyone over the age of fifteen was expected to pay 12d as a poll tax although those who were wealthier could pay more to cover those less fortunate. Eleven households listed in the Dorking return seem to consist of husband, wife and one or two *serviens*. In eight of these, the relationship can be deduced by the fact that the *serviens* is named next in the list, after the husband and wife, and that the master of the house paid most of the tax. For example, Adam at Homwode paid 2s 8d: 12d for him and 12d for his wife, Isabelle, plus an extra 8d. The *serviens*, Wiliam at Dene, then paid the remaining 4d. In the other three such households, the *serviens* was specifically described as 'his serving man' (*serviens eius*) and was not given a surname, which might suggest he was living in. Indeed, they may have been part of the family: *serviens* was sometimes used to signify a son or daughter still living at home and legally the responsibility of his or her parents. This was the case with Peter at Monte, described as *serviens* and listed directly after William at Monte and his wife Letice.[166] (William paid 2s 8d and Peter 4d.) Robert, the son of Adam and Agnes Clerk, was described as both *filius eius* and *serviens*. (Confusingly, he may have been married: two women, Alice and Margery, were described as the 'wife of Robert Clerk' but both were named at the end of the Dorking return, when there was evidently some catching up being done. One 'Robert Clerk' was a holder of land; the other was the son of Adam and Agnes.)

---

[166] In the accounts for 1386-7, Peter is described as William's son; he, his father and his brother Walter were all paying chevage.

Most of these *serviens* were single but there were exceptions. Thomas Smyth and his wife Matilda were both described as *serviens*, as was Henry at Monte, who was married to Edith. Henry paid 2s 4d for them both, which is 4d more than required, so his position is difficult to establish. Isabelle Taylor and William Taylor paid their 2s together but it's not known what their relationship was or whether they were part of the household of John Taylor and his wife, Edith, who appear next in the list.

Ten people were described in the Dorking return as *servient*. They appear in five pairs: William Mum, Robert at Sonde and William Tanner were named with their wives, all of whom were called Alice. John Coker and William Coker paid 12d together; they may have worked for John and Matilda at Dene (although John Coker is also listed as one of John Tannere's dependants). John and William's relationship is unknown. Details from the court rolls don't support the idea that these people were servants as such and they certainly weren't labourers. Perhaps they worked for someone else in a different capacity? The final pair of *servients* were called Isabelle and Ralph and were listed without surnames directly after a holder of land called Alice at Sonde. Perhaps they were her live-in servants? Alice may have paid part of their tax: she contributed 18d, while they jointly paid 12d.

Although Dorking had increased in importance as a market-town, the land was still the primary way to sustain a family on the manor. The poll tax return lists 48 *terre tenente* and 39 *laborarii*; the former means 'holder of land' while the latter can mean 'labourer' or 'smallholder'. The *terre tenente* include many names which one would expect, such as John at Chert, Roger Ashcombe and several members of the Sonde family. Among the *laborarii*, Joan Brekespere, William Brekespere, John Bruggesulle, William Bruggesulle and Richard Spycer are most likely to be smallholders.[167] Eleven of those listed as *laborarii* feature in the court rolls as 'common labourers', which presumably means they were hiring out their labour. Meanwhile, the court rolls confirm that John Bal, snr and William Whyte were the holders of cotlands, while John Coytere and Thomas Tournour were described as a tanner and a turner respectively. Twenty-four of the

---

[167] The published return clearly says 'Joanna' rather than 'Joannes' Brekespere.

laborarii are listed in the return without any spouse. However, that doesn't necessarily mean they weren't married: for example, Roger Pypyn had a wife called Alice who was mentioned in the 1382 court roll. Perhaps they got married after the inspectors had passed through the district.

We can't tell which of the *terre tenente* and *laborarii* held the customary tenancies, not least because, by this period, it was not unusual for several plots to be held by one tenant. However, the Grenehurst tenement, which had been alienated in 1344, was the cause of some confusion in 1381. The court roll recorded that the half-virgate had 'returned to the lord's hand', having been held by the late John Kyngesfolde, and that heriot was due. Then, on the 12th May, Alice, daughter of Giles Taillor, came to court with a deed which showed that she held the land, having been granted it by a Roger Holm and several others. She swore fealty for the property, which was granted a few years later to Hugh and Joan Netelfold by Giles Taillor, Thomas Rolf and John White. At that point, the tenement comprised one messuage, 73 acres of land, three acres of meadow, 20 acres of wood and 24 acres of pasture. 5d rent and a red rose were due annually and the tenement was transferred on receipt of 100 marks in silver. [168]

John Kyngesfold was, as we have seen, lord of Paddington manor and patron of Robert Snokeshull, vicar of Abinger. He also served as MP for Surrey and was steward to the earl in 1380, being referred to as such in the 1381-2 accounts. He died in August 1381; his Inquisition Post Mortem refers to land in Buckinghamshire which he had granted to Roger Holm, a canon of St Paul's, William de Newdigate, Robert Snokeshull and others at Michaelmas, 1375. [169] Presumably, he had done the same with his Surrey property and these were the men who then granted Grenehurst to Alice, daughter of Giles Taillor. Part of the delay in sorting the matter out may have been due to the fact that Alice lived at Kingsfold rather than in Dorking; her father was described elsewhere as being 'of Kingsfold'. [170] According to the court roll for 1381-2, John Kyngesfold also held the Wadelshurst tenancy at the time of his death but this was as inaccurate as

---

[168] Pedes Finium, p.156 (23).
[169] CIPM, vol 15, pp.202-217 (509).
[170] Pedes Finium, p.223 (164).

the court's information on Grenehurst: John Wadelshurst surrendered it the following year, in a swap for land held by William at Monte and his wife, Letice.

We might expect the poll tax return to give us a clear idea of who lived in the manor, including as it should all adults over the age of fifteen, regardless of status or income. Unfortunately, the return has a reputation among historians for unreliability as a source for population figures because avoidance was higher than usual. The government sent out commissioners in March 1381 to investigate whether the tax had been assessed and collected properly. Surrey was not one of the counties investigated, which suggests that the problems were less marked here. That said, there are one or two obvious omissions in the Dorking section, although a few of these 'missing persons' can be found in the nearby manors of Ockley or Milton. Westcott was now large enough to be listed separately by the poll tax inspectors. The settlement was obviously developing its own identity, as one of the defendants in a trespass case at the manor court was described as being 'of Westkot'.

Most surprisingly, William Upbroke, the reeve, doesn't appear in the return. Unfortunately, this means we don't know his wife's name or any other details about his household or how he would have described his occupation or position. John Broman and John Godwyne, who both appear in the court roll regarding their tenements, are also missing. Like William Upbroke, they were personally unfree and were not paying chevage, so they must have been living on the manor. Another surprising absentee is John at Honchones, aleseller, aletaster and affeerer at the manor court. In his case, we know he was married because he died a couple of years later and his widow, Agnes, was his executrix.

John Syre was a tenant of part of the Ewekene, responsible for road repairs next to his property. His wife, Joan, paid her poll tax but he did not (despite Joan being referred to in the return as 'the wife of John Syre'). Conversely, several women dodged the tax, including Margery, the wife of Richard Skynnere, and Joan, the wife of Richard Spycer. Matilda Bourere is also missing, despite unjustly raising the hue and cry against John at Honchones and so, presumably, living in the town. Alice at Bregge, from whom John Shepherde (himself resident at Milton) acquired six acres of land in the Homwode, might also be expected to appear in the return. Perhaps unsurprisingly, Joan Frowe, who had some disreputable connection with John Carpenter, jnr, did not pay the poll tax. Felicia and Matilda Suel, who we only know about because they were involved in fights, are also missing.

Mobility increased after the Black Death, particularly for work. The Dorking poll tax return seems to reflect that, as it includes a number of names not seen previously on the manor. Among the *serviens*, Matilda Laurence, John Peverell, John Sneller, Margery Sorel and Alice Stonere are new arrivals. Among the *laborarii*, Henry Aroun, John Coytere, William Person, William Peverell and John Walshe are likewise. Matheus Wyvenhoe was a tailor who had arrived by 1365, while the new miller was named as Thomas Snodwyne. Movement went the other way, too. John Brokere, Richard Brokere and the sons of William at Monte all paid chevage in 1381-2 and seven other men asked to be released from suit of court, perhaps because they were working away from the manor.[171]

One useful aspect of the poll tax is that it includes the names of many wives, who appear rarely in manorial documentation. The return for Dorking names 93 wives out of a total of 279 residents. The names of these women are mostly as one would expect: Agnes, Alice, Amice, Avelina, Christina, Dionisia, Edith, Isabelle, Joan, Juliana, Margery, Matilda and Rose. However, they also include some new arrivals: Beatrix, Emma, Felicia, Katherine, Letice, Milsant and Petronilla. ('Gunnild' seems to have fallen out of favour, although the wife of Thomas Garlond, living in Ockley, was so called.)

Only eight sons or daughters were specifically named as such in the Dorking return. The daughter was Edith, whose parents were John Upbroke, one of the *terre tenente*, and Isabelle. Their son, John, had obviously died before 1381 as his father served as his executor. John also paid 6s 8d so that Edith could be married where he chose; this is the family

---

[171] They were: William at Dene, John Godefray, William Kymere, William Pirye, Thomas Rede, Robert at Risbrugge and Thomas Rolf.

that had suffered the scandal of another daughter's relationship with John Gostrode seveteen years earlier.

Another scandal came to light in 1381-2, when it was presented at the manor court that Avelina Noble, who held the cotland called Trasshes for 4s, was on the point of death. Her son John came to ask to be admitted to the cotland but was refused because he was a bastard. Bastardy was rare in medieval society, where girls married relatively young and marriage was universal. Indeed, in the hundred-year period studied in this book, only four cases have come to light: Emma, wife of Peter de Newdigate, Lucy de Ewekene and the above-mentioned John. The fourth is that of Ralph Bochiere (also known as 'le Rede'). He was father of a daughter called Emma, in which capacity he appeared in the Extent and a contemporary property deed.[172] His illegitimacy was revealed in 1384 due to a property dispute amongst his descendants, when John Bal, jnr and his wife, Alice, and William Mum and his wife, also called Alice, claimed admittance to the 300 acres of meadowland which had been Thomas Rede's. Their claim was thrown out because it was via Ralph, who was brother to Thomas but a bastard, his mother's name not being known.

One family matter which dominated the court rolls for 1381-2 and 1382-3 was an inheritance dispute regarding Richard, son and heir of Richard at Sonde. He was obviously underage, his guardians being the attorneys Nicholas Henle and Henry at Sonde. The earl seems to have claimed the boy's wardship: the matter was raised in the manor court on 25th November 1381 and then went on for at least two years. Land and tenements were retained in the earl's hand and a goblet taken into safe custody but neither guardian appeared at court, despite repeated summonses.

---

[172] BL 18581.

How to Make a Living

If Avelina, wife of Stephen at Holoweye, came to Dorking on market-day to do some shopping, who would she have done business with? If she were buying provisions for her household, then she might have bought meat from one of the five butchers in the town: Robert Henle, William Inchered, John Noble, Thomas Noble or Richard Skynnere. William Inchered also sold bread, alongside Alice Kene, Walter Kene and Roger Yonge; wastelbread, cocketbread and wholebread were available to the Dorking housewife. For fish, Avelina could go to John A Neve or John Fisher.

If Avelina had lived in the town, she might have bought her food from one of the hucksters now operating in Dorking. Hucksters were women who bought goods at market and then touted them round a town, selling directly to people at home. This may not sound very controversial but it aroused the ire of the authorities; like forestalling, it was seen as an unfair way of competing with the honest housewife and of putting up prices. The butchers appear to have been particularly involved. In 1381, Margery, wife of Richard Skynnere, was fined for selling bread in this way; the following year, she and Dionisia, wife of Willian Inchered, were cited for the same offence. The official name for this re-selling was 'regrating', for which Robert Henle was fined alongside Margery in 1381. Both were also prosecuted for selling underweight bread, which may explain some of the authorities' antipathy to the practice.

If Avelina sought shoes or clothing, she could have tried John Bemond or John Dauwe, the cobblers, or John Ode, the draper. There were also four tailors: John Godefray, Roger Kempe, Richard Pynshagh and Matheus Wyvenhoe. Indeed, the textile trade seems to have increased dramatically in Dorking. Five full-time weavers were named in the poll tax return: Roger Bacheler, Richard Busche, William Kymere, Gilbert Olyne and Thomas Webbe. However, there were many more working in the town. The court roll also names Agnes Bacheler, Margery Busche, Alice Pynshawe, the wife of William Tanner, John Walshe and Harry Webbe. As Agnes and Margery's husbands were weavers, they probably worked as part of the family firm; Alice Pynshawe's husband was a tailor. Laurence Ingleby, the fuller, was also still plying his trade in Dorking.

Alternatively, Avelina might visit one of the twelve women who were described in the poll tax return as a 'spinster' (*filater*). Although married women could make their living through spinning or sewing, the role tended to be filled by single women, often living alone and working independently. This was another recent development that caused the authorities in many towns unease. The Dorking spinsters were all listed individually in the poll tax return but they came from local families: their names were Emma Bradele, Agnes at Bourne, Dionisia Caas, Alice Cok, Isabelle at Flusshe, Katherine Fust, Alice at Hambreche, Beatrix Kene, Matilda Noble, Leticia Pouke, Alice Proteriche and Alice Pype. None of these women came to the official attention of the manor court, so we know no more about them. However, according to the 1381-2 court roll, there was also a 'huckster of wool' in Dorking: our old friend, Joan Frowe.[173] Perhaps she sold wool to the town's spinsters.

The building trade was booming. There were six carpenters (Walter Bakere, John Inwyn, Thomas at Lompulle, John Lyne, William Lythiere and Robert at Shete) and two smiths (William Caas and Richard Smyth). William Patterne was described as a tiler of houses and John Masoun was, as we have seen, the mason. He seems to have been doing quite well, paying 6s 8d for permission to quarry freestone during a seven-year period on villein land held by John Coker. This was fine-grained stone

Two women spinning and carding wool.

---

[173] The only other Frowes the author has found lived in Southwark. Perhaps Joan, a new arrival in the town, had migrated from there (Fenwick (2001), pt 2, p.562).

which could be cut in any direction, making it suitable for ornamental work. Other trades also flourished. Thomas Tournour was, unsurprisingly, the turner, while the continuing war in France might account for the presence of no less than three fletchers: John Averay, John Bonet and John Dyfforde.

Two millers operating in Dorking were called William Pype and Thomas Snodwyne. Their mills must have been upstream of the tanneries, whose owners were named in the court rolls as John Noble and John Tannere. John Noble had an established business, although perhaps not a very well-run one: in January 1375/6, he had been among seven tanners whose pieces of leather were presented as being badly tanned by six governors of the Cordwainers Company.[174] The tanners acknowledged their guilt and were forgiven and bound over. (To be fair, the leather was being judged against a recent ordinance, so perhaps they had been caught out by a change in the rules.) In the poll tax return, John Noble was named on his own, while John Tannere appeared with his wife, Joan, son, Richard, and (possibly) the aforementioned John Coker as a *serviens*. Both tanners were fined at the manor court for breaking the assize on labour. John Tannere was also an aleseller and was repeatedly summoned to court for breaking the pannage restrictions; he was also required to explain why he hadn't taken his corn to the earl's mill, as was expected of a customary tenant. He had a shop, which was claimed by his daughter and heiress, Joan, wife of Richard Ware of Leatherhead, in 1382.

There seems to have been some kind of trouble among the tanners. Roger Bacheler, who was a weaver, was also cited in the manor court for breaking the assize, when he was described as a tanner of hides. Meanwhile, in the 1381-2 View of Frankpledge, John Noble was fined for assaulting Agnes, Roger's wife. Perhaps John resented Roger moving into the tanning trade? At the same View, it was presented that John had come into Dorking six months earlier, against the peace, and broken into John Tannere's close, taking away tanned hides. It's not clear what all this adds up to but it feels like there was friction between the various tanners operating in Dorking. In addition, two people were named in the View as

---

[174] Letter Book H, p.23.

regraters of hides (Christopher Clerk and Katherine Spicer). Why there should be a need for this is unclear.

The poll tax included ten brewers: John Bal, jnr, Thomas Caas, Stephen Deyere, William Elmeshale, John Henhurst, Richard Henhurst, Alice Kene, William Palmere, Elizabeth at Sonde and Adam Whytyng. There's no correlation between these names and those who were fined at the manor court for breaking the assize: Stephen Deyere, Richard Henhurst and Elizabeth at Sonde weren't fined at all and Adam Whytyng only once. However, those most frequently fined included John Bal, jnr, Thomas Caas, Alice Kene and William Palmere. They all paid the fee seven or more times, as did Richard Bussh, Nicholas Henle, Laurence Ingelby, John A Neve and Roger Yonge. A total of 48 alesellers were named in the 1381-2 court roll, significantly fewer than in previous years, and only two of them were women: Alice Kene and a Catherine of Leatherhead (who only appears once). This might suggest an increased professionalism in the trade, pushing out the home-based female selling her surplus brew, which would not be unexpected in this period. Three innkeepers were named in the View of Frankpledge as selling victuals and making too much profit: William Coupere, Adam Whytyng and Roger Yonge. Only William was called an innkeeper in the poll tax return; he never appears in the aletasters' lists, which might suggest he was buying ale from others rather than brewing it himself. Adam and Roger were both described as 'brewers' in the poll tax return.

For the first time, we have a reference to cider being sold in the town. Robert Henle and Henry at Sonde were cited at court for selling two pipes of cider at 2d per gallon and taking excessive profits of 16s. Both men were fined 6d. It's not known whether the cider was brewed locally; the only contemporary reference to orchard fruit of which the author is aware occurred in the accounts of 1383, when 'no apples or pears were sold, they failing throughout the country'.[175] There was also a piece of land called 'Perry Field' on the outskirts of town, near the Sonde property.[176]

---

[175] Quoted by Bray (1816), p.285. The original set of accounts no longer exist.
[176] See BL 18613.

The Church

John Appletone was appointed vicar of Dorking on 11th June 1378. Six years later, he swapped benefices with William Crese and went to Ewhurst; William stayed until 1391, when he was replaced by Stephen Balcome. Meanwhile, in 1371, William le Haze resigned from the vicarage at Effingham in order to take up that of Capel. By 1381, he had been replaced or joined by John Dalby, who was described in the Dorking court roll as 'chaplain of Capel'.

Unfortunately, John Dalby's time on the manor doesn't seem to have been a very happy one. During the court year of 1381-2, he brought pleas of debt against twenty different defendants, most of whom hailed from the south of the manor.[177] The sums owed varied between 1s and 15s 10d and one complaint dated back to Michaelmas of the previous year; in that case, the defendant, William at Hulle, waged his law. Why the chaplain should suddenly call in all these debts is not clear. Perhaps he was leaving the parish: the court rolls subsequently refer to Thomas Hayton as chaplain of Capel and John Dalby pursued these debts through his attorney, Nicholas Henle, rather than in person. In March of 1382/3, he raised another plea against William Inchered regarding 12s 6d in principal, plus 6d damages. It could be that these were private debts: it wasn't unusual for clergy to lend money, although chaplains weren't very well paid, so perhaps this is unlikely.[178]

One of John's pledges in 1381-2 was William Elmeshale. He also appeared later in the court roll in connection with two cases where each defendant acknowledged that he owed money for the stipend of one chaplain, which should have been paid to William and his servant. Neither defendant (Roger Bacheler and Thomas Caas) was one of those being pursued for debt by John Dalby but this might shed some light on matters.

---

[177] They were: Richard Brekespere, William Brekespere, John Bruggesulle, William Bruggesulle, John Bourere, John Charesmore, Thomas Charesmore, Walter Charesmore, William at Hulle, John Hunte, Thomas Gerlonde of Ockley, Roger Langshete, Adam at Lythe, Walter Peyter, Robert Risbrugge, Thomas Rogger, William Rykeman, John Sawere, Richard Sket and John Wadelshurst (who also owed a bushel of wheat).

[178] See McIntosh (1988).

Perhaps, rather than private debts, this money represented unpaid dues? The court roll for 1384-5 included more pleas of debt raised by John Dalby, this time against John Charesmore, John at Hale, John Hulle, Roger Langshete, Adam Lythe and Richard Sket and his wife Matilda. In the latter case, Richard and Matilda waged their law because they said that Matilda had paid 3s 4d to an officer of the bishop of Winchester, so they didn't owe it to John Dalby. The manor court accepted their version of events and fined John 2d for a false plaint. It's tempting to make a connection with contemporary political events: lollards objected to the payment of tithes, especially by the poor, and the issue had been vociferously raised by John Ball, the priest associated with the Peasants' Revolt.

In the View of Frankpledge for 1381-2, 'John, chaplain of Dorking' was indicted for assaulting Stephen Baker. The court roll of 1384-5 also dealt with two incidents which had happened the previous year. Firstly, John 'lately chaplain of Dorking parish' was accused of beating up and making threats to William at Dene, the beadle, when the latter was 'occupied about the execution of commands pertaining to his office'. This had occurred on the 15th October 1383; John admitted the charge and was fined 3s 4d. Secondly, there was a dispute between Alice Kene and 'John, lately chaplain of Dorking parish' over various goods that she had lent him the year before: a tablecloth worth 3s 4d, a towel worth 12d and a bronze pot worth 2s 6d. John was present in court to deny the charge but subsequently defaulted, so Alice won her claim for 13s 4d (the price of the goods plus 6s 8d in damages). It's not clear whether this was the same man as John Dalby; given that he is not specifically named as such and was present in the court (rather than represented by an attorney), it may be a different man. Either way, relations between clergy and laity in the manor seem to have become rather fraught.

The Wider World

In the 1370s, a 'Great Rumour' was being spread among manorial tenants in southern England. The rumour suggested that, if a manor had once belonged to the king (known as 'ancient demesne'), the tenants should be free of all obligations apart from rent and suit of court. Proof would be provided by the relevant entry in Domesday Book. On at least forty manors, tenants clubbed together to raise funds for an 'exemplification': a document, issued by the king, containing the Domesday information for the manor they worked on.[179]

This wasn't a new idea. Since at least the 1280s, such requests had been made by tenants who felt their current landlord was unlawfully increasing the services they owed. Domesday Book was held in great respect by English tenants and they had long memories. For instance, some tenants of Chertsey Abbey appealed to a series of deeds issued by Anglo-Saxon kings to prove their point.[180] However, the new development in the 1380s was the idea that *all* customary services might be dispensed with on an 'ancient demesne' estate. It was being spread by 'counsellors, maintainers and abettors' who encouraged tenants to apply to Chancery and arranged the business for them.[181] This could lead to serious trouble. On four Surrey manors held by Chertsey Abbey, long-standing tension led to riots: the tenants had bought an exemplification and refused to work for the abbey, threatening to burn it down if they had to. When the sheriff of Surrey was called in, his men were nearly killed.

Obviously, this sort of thing didn't go down well with the authorities. A series of royal commissions were set up to investigate these 'confederations'; the Surrey one was led by Robert Bealknapp, the chief justice, and included Robert Loxle, royal escheator and several times MP for Surrey, and John Kyngesfold.[182] A subsequent commission to investigate the Chertsey Abbey tenants included the same men, plus other worthies

---

[179] See Faith (1987).

[180] The deeds had in fact been forged years earlier but the point is that the tenants knew about them.

[181] CPR RII, vol I, p.251.

[182] CPR RII, vol I, p.50.

such as Nicholas Carew. It was led by Richard, Earl of Arundel.[183] Interestingly, Dorking's tenants did not go down this route, despite the fact that Dorking had once been a royal manor. It may be that they benefitted from having such a distant landlord, unlike those on the notoriously well-run monastic estates.

Dispensing justice through royal commissions was one of the sources of popular resentment in this period, sidelining as it did the hundred and royal courts. The same names, including those mentioned above, occur repeatedly during the 1370s and 80s on commissions of the peace and those set up to deal with the aftermath of the 'Peasants' Revolt'. The earl was involved with commissions in both Surrey and Sussex to suppress unlawful assemblies and punish the rebels. In March 1382, a proclamation was circulated to be read out to all congregations, condemning the 'treasonable hostile rising of divers evildoers' and threatening the arrest of any rebels or those who incited rebellion, with suppression of meetings and confiscation of goods.[184]

Another source of resentment was, of course, the heavy burden of taxation. The poll tax of 1381 was the third in a quick succession of such taxes. It was also the least equitable. Agreed, eventually, by Parliament in November 1380, on the 7th December commissioners were appointed to assess the tax in each county and to oversee the process. John Kyngesfold was one of the assessors.[185]

The events of the summer of 1381 are well known. The closest the trouble got to Dorking was at Guildford, where records were burned and rebels stole £25 10s collected towards the farm of the shire.[186] Guildford castle was the county gaol for both Surrey and Sussex but there's no evidence that it was stormed, unlike the earl's castle at Lewes. There, a number of armed men broke the gates, doors and windows of the castle, threw down buildings and consumed and destroyed ten casks of wine, valued at £100. They also burned the earl's rolls, rentals and other

---

[183] CPR RII, vol I, p.251.
[184] CPR RII, vol II, p.138.
[185] CFR RII, vol I, pp.224-5.
[186] VCH Surrey, vol I, p.362.

muniments.[187] Perhaps the Dorking records were being kept at Lewes, which might account for their patchy survival before the 1380s. Arundel castle was also attacked. Many rebels were imprisoned at Guildford; so many that Earl Richard applied for permission to move some of them to his castles at Arundel and Lewes.[188] However, the problems at Guildford continued: in October 1382, five prisoners escaped. One was recaptured but the others sought the sanctuary of the church and then left the country.[189]

One final point. In December 1384, Nicholas Henle (the attorney) received all the land and tenements formerly held by his brother, Thomas, who had lately been condemned and outlawed. The author has been unable to discover what he had done; it's tempting to put it down to his being a rebel but it could just be an unpaid debt.

[187] CPR RII, vol II, p.259.
[188] CPR RII, vol II, p.73.
[189] CPR RII, vol II, p.181. The sheriff was pardoned at the earl's request.

Epilogue

Earl Richard, who inherited his father's lands and titles in 1376, was the fourth Earl of Arundel. His brother, Thomas, was bishop of Ely, becoming archbishop of York between 1388-97 and then archbishop of Canterbury. At the coronation of Richard II, Earl Richard carried the crown but his close ties with the Duke of Gloucester, the king's uncle, ultimately led to trouble. They were dismissed from the royal council in 1387, when the king packed it with his cronies. Summoned to a meeting, Gloucester and Arundel raised troops and defeated the new council at Radcot Bridge on the 22nd December 1387. The following year's Merciless Parliament condemned the king's favourites and, by 1394, the earl was once more a member of the council. However, he quarrelled with John of Gaunt and insulted the king by being late for the queen's funeral. He was arrested on the 12th July 1397.

The earl was executed on the 21st September of the same year. All his land and property was confiscated and an Inquisition Post Mortem listed everything he held on or after the 19th November 1386.[190] This document's description of Dorking manor seems rather inaccurate: the acreages of land available for arable, pasture, meadow and woods were significantly underestimated. Compared with the manorial accounts for 1386-7, the amounts due as rent from customary tenancies, mills, warren, court perks and other sources were also much less than they should have been. One wonders who supplied the information.

The impact of the earl's fall can be seen in the Dorking manorial records. In 1396-7, the demesne land was demised at farm to Henry at Sonde and Richard at Sonde, who took it for seven years. The stock, including the dairy herd, had been sold the previous year. The Sondes paid £6 13s 4d per year until 1420-1, when Richard Charesmore leased the land on the same terms, followed by John Brekespere in 1426-7. Presumably, it wasn't a very profitable investment: the following year, the demesne was parcelled up into seven different blocks, which were leased out separately.

The market and mills were also becoming less profitable and therefore more difficult to lease. Nicholas Henle refused the mills in 1384, despite

---

[190] CIM, vol V, p.213.

having taken them the previous year. They were then managed directly until at least 1389, when it was reported that £10 13s 4d was 'received of the farm of the mill and tolls of the market of Dorking, no demand this year'. John Ode and Nicholas Henle took them on in 1391-2 for four years, followed by John Carpenter, jnr. Part the problem may have stemmed from a lack of maintentance: in 1396-7, a major programme of repairs took place at the Medmell and the floodgates, involving extraction of old timbers and replacement with new, plus some serious earthworks and scouring of the millpond. The cost was over £27 and John Carpenter received a rebate for the eleven weeks the mill was out of action. The following year, William Elmeshale and William Palmere leased mills and market for seven years, paying £10 6s 8d per year.

The last of the manorial assets to be leased out was the warren. Receipts from sales of rabbits varied in the first ten years of the 15thC between 40s for 192 to 100s for 480 (a particularly good year). The warrener's wages had gone up in 1390 to 1½d a day (from 1d), so 41s 5½d would have been deducted from warren profits to pay him. Perhaps this is what prompted the decision to farm the warren out. In 1413-14, Henry at Sonde, Robert at Sonde, Thomas Asshurst and Robert Ashcombe took it for £6 13s 4d per year 'for the lifetime of the current earl'. By 1419-20, the lease had been taken over by Richard Sket and John Lythiere; in 1427-8, it lay with Gilbert Cartere. They paid the same rate, which seems rather a lot.

As part of the process in 1396-7, a new rental was drawn up and examined by one of the king's auditors. Although the document doesn't survive, it evidently showed that large numbers of properties were 'in the lord's hand' and specifically referred to the 'lack of rent of divers places lying in the vill of Dorking'. It sounds like the population of Dorking had dropped, which wouldn't be a surprise as the effect of the Black Death really took hold in the 15thC. The numbers of unlet properties also suggest that the bottom had dropped out of the Dorking property market. By the 1420s, it was common for several customary tenancies to be held by one person, such as Robert Pleystowe, who held the neighbouring properties of Pleystowe, Rushett and Hacche. When Richard Sket renewed his lease on the market and mills in 1407-8, he only paid £7 13s 9d 'for scarcity of people in the district'; eighteen years later, when the market and mills were demised to William Brekespere and Richard Haye, respectively, the market was only worth 6s 8d and the mills £6 6s 8d. Perhaps it was then that the market became weekly, held only on a Thursday. It's all in marked contrast to the sums set out in the Extent, when the market had been valued at £12 and the mills at £11 11s 8d.

Some families obviously decided their future lay elsewhere. John Brokere and Richard Brokere both paid chevage between 1386-7 and 1393-4. William at Monte left in 1386-7, along with both his sons, Walter and Peter. Peter made the move permanent: from 1396-7 onwards, he was described as 'staying in London', for which he paid extra. Walter at Pleystowe paid chevage between 1393-4 and 1413-14; however, Thomas Pleystowe left the manor in 1422 without permission, for which the homage was fined 20s.

The Brekesperes were sailing close to the wind, as ever. In 1418-19, John Brekespere occupied his father William's tenement without permission; William had also leased a messuage and two fields to William Pakyn without licence. Two years later, William had left the manor and the buildings at Upper Brekesperes and Nether Brekesperes were reported as ruinous. All his tenements were confiscated, although he did subsequently return to the manor. Walter Arnold, John Bourere, Henry Oldryk, John Proterych and Richard Sket were also reported for having derelict buildings.

However, it wasn't all doom and gloom. Of the nine men who leased the divided demesne in 1427-8, five had names we haven't seen previously on the manor. Presumably, they had moved to Dorking or thought is worth investing in the place. A number of Londoners' wills surviving from the mid-15thC include bequests to Dorking church and, often, a wish to be buried in the churchyard. Henry Wolford left 10 marks to help buy a 'great bell' for the bell-tower 'whenever the parishioners of the church of Dorking should wish to order and buy' it. (If they failed to do so after two or three years, the money was to be distributed among various charities.) Henry Sonde asked to be buried next to his father, Robert, and left money for candles for the 'light there called Our Lady light' and the light of St John, plus an ox to the Dorking Brotherhood and 'a great log for making the steps leading to the bell tower of the same church'. In 1489, John Meryden left five marks for the fabric of the church in which he was baptised and, the following year, Richard Wodde left a cow worth 6s 8d in order to repair 'a certain glass window on the west side of the said church of Dorking'.[191] Like Peter at Monte, these men had been drawn to London but they evidently didn't forget their home parish.

Meanwhile, the ties that bound those who were personally unfree were weakening. In 1422-3, Isabelle Langshete gave 6s 8d to marry where she chose; Joan Brekespere did the same four years later. The numbers of people paying to skip attendance at court had reached as high as twenty-three in 1384 and stayed at that level: in 1400, it was twenty-seven. From the 1420s onward, the customary tenants paid 40s per year to avoid having to transport timber to Kingston; conversely, at some point, payment in lieu for customary labour was dropped. This seems to have taken place before 1440, as the Inquisition Post Mortem of the Countess Beatrice makes no mention of it.[192] However, some dues went on being paid: as late as 1921, fines, heriots, quitrents and wayleaves were still being collected from the remaining eleven customary tenancies.[193] Borough English also still applied on the manor; all were abolished in 1922, when copyhold tenure was brought to an end in England.

In 1400, Earl Thomas was restored to his father's honours and lands by the new king Henry IV. The Dorking View of Frankpledge for that year records that the whole homage swore that all was well on the manor; they were given a day to make the usual oath to their new lord, while all free tenants were distrained to make fealty. When the earl died in 1415, he left three sisters as his heirs. His widow, Beatrice, held Dorking manor as her dower until her death and then the manor was divided. By the time of the 1649 survey, everything was split between the Earl of Arundel (who held three quarters) and Sir Ambrose Brown (who held the other quarter). Although most of the families we have been following had disappeared from the manorial records by the time of the 1649 survey, their names live on in locations and farms that survive to this day. The information we

---

[191] PROB 11/3/362, PROB 11/5/121, PROB 11/8/432 & DW/PA/7/002 f.iid.
[192] CIPM, vol XXV, p.324.
[193] DM S1603.

glean from the manorial records can give us a glimpse of part of their lives but, inevitably, much remains obscure. That being said, next time you drive past Redlands Lane, think of Thomas Rede and his 300 acres; imagine the Godwynes farming what is now the Goodwyns estate or the widow Sybil ruling the roost at Brekesperes farm.

Appendix A

Well-to-do Dorking tenants from whose rent £20 was taken in 1311 for Sir John de Wysham, arranged alphabetically (CPR Ed II, vol I, p.405).

Name	Amount		Name	Amount	
	s	d		s	d
William Aguilon	17		Gilbert at Hulle	2	6
Walter Alard	10	10	William Kene	2	
Peter de Ashcombe	6	6	William de Langshete	12	
Richard de Ashcombe	2		Agnes, widow of Robert at Lese	2	
Thomas de Ashcombe	2	11½	Hugh Lovel & Ralph de Hengham	47	4½
Robert Avery	2	6	Walter de Lutresford	2	6
Ralph Bonet	2	6	Walter Mum	5	10
Adam at Brugge & John, his brother	12		William Orpedeman	3	6
Agnes at Byse	3	9	Laurence de Oxenford	2	9
Peter le Cartere	2	9	Agnes, widow of Robert Page	5	
Nicholas Chapman	2	9	John, son of Robert Page	3	
Roger at Chert	4	6	Hugh at Pleystowe	12	
Thomas at Churchgate	12	8¾	Robert at Pleystowe	6	
Walter at Churchgate	2		John Pouke	2	¾
William Degere, jnr	9	6½	The Prioress of Kilburn	3	6
Robert Deth	4	3½	Matilda, daughter of Richard le Smyth	5	
Maurice de Ewekene	22		Robert at Sonde	12	9
Clerekyn de Florence	52	3	Adam Stub	2	6
Thomas at Flushe	2	6	Robert Upbroke	6	
Odo at Garston	2	6	Tenants of the land of Wadelshurst	12	
Walter at Hambreche	5	1½	Nicholas de Weston	29	3
William Harm	2		John White	7	5
Robert de Heghland	3	11	Peter Willeman	4	10
Henry at Hethe	9	7	William de Wynterfold	3	
Gilbert at Hok	2	3	Henry, son of William Whytyng	2	
William at Homwode	2	6			

Appendix B

1332 lay subsidy return for the 'vill de Dorkyng', arranged alphabetically, author's corrections in square brackets (SRS XI, pp.31-2).

Name	Amount s	Amount d	Name	Amount s	Amount d
Roger Aleyn		13	John Coupere		8
Robert de Ashcombe		8	Robert Decht [Deth]		17¾
John Baron		9¾	Peter at Dene		8
Thomas Belamy		12	Gunnild de Ewekene	2	
Adam le Belde		9¾	Maurice de Ewekene		8
John le Belde		12	Thomas at Flushe	2	8
Roger at Berne [Bourne]		8	William le Fust		8
John le Blak'		12	William le Fyssher'		16
Peter Blandys		8	Peter Godard		8
Robert Bonet		13¾	William le Goldsmyth		8
Robert le Bourere		12	Richard at Hacche		16
William Bradele		20	Robert at Heghelond		8
Richard Brekespere	2		Richard de Henle, jnr		8
Robert at Brok'		8	Richard de Henle, snr		8
William Bronnot	3		Alice Hurlewyne		8
William de Brug'		8	Gilbert Hychecok'		9¾
John de Brugesull'		12¾	Richard le Ismongere		19¼
Richard le Brut		22½	Henry de Langeshete		12
Roger Buksmere		16	Roger de Langshete		12
Adam Carpe[n]ter		8	William le Lythyer'		12
Nicholas le Cartere		16	Walter Marchant		8
John Chaloner		16	William Marchant		8
John le Chapman		8	Hugh at Medende		16
Thomas at Chergate	2	7¼	Robert at Monte	2	
Henry at Clause? [Chert]		8	Jul' Monim [Mum]		16
Richard de Clerk'		16	Robert Noble	4	
Robert le Clerk'	2	¼	William Ode		8
Richard Coker		9	Henry Oliue [Olyne]		8
William Coker		12	Henry Page		8
John Coleman	4	¾	Richard Peter		8
Peter Comber'		12	Stephen Peter		8
Thomas de Compeden'		17	Robert at Pleystowe	3	¾

Appendix B - continued

Name	Amount	
	s	**d**
Is' at Pleystowe [Isabelle?]	2	
John Pouk'		12
Peter Priut	2	
Thomas le Rede	2	4
Thomas Rolf	2	2
William Rolf	2	1
Henry Ropere		8
Richard at Rugge		17¾
William at Rysbrug'		20
William le Sket		18
Adam at Sonde		8
Edward at Sonde	2	
Robert at Sonde	8	3½
Roger at Sonde		8
Peter Spicer		8
Ralph Spicer		8
Richard Sprot		18½
John Stanston'		9
Elias de Stombelhale		14½
Hugh at Strode	2	
John Stub	2	
Ralph Stub	2	
Thomas le Tailur		12
Adam le Tanner'		8
Gilbert le Tanner'	3	
John Trycoys	2	
Robert de Upbrok	2	7¼
Stephen de Wadelehurst	3	11
John de Warenne	7	
Peter at Watere		8
Robert le Weston'	5	11¼
William le Wreche		8

Appendix C

The new lords of Dorking and the freeholders who swore fealty to them in 1365. Holders of customary tenancies and cottars also swore but were not named. Freeholders have been listed alphabetically but the lords have been left in order of precedence.

Name of lord	
Sir John, Duke of Lancaster	Sir Walter de Upton
Sir Humphrey le Bohun, Earl of Hereford	Sir Edward St John
Sir Henry Beamond	Sir John de Ludlow
Sir Roger Lestraunge	William Banastre
Sir Guy de Brian	Robert Hailsham
Sir Warin de Lisle	John Butler
Sir Henry Percy	Roger Dalyngrugge
Sir Thomas de Ludlow	John Kyngesfolde
Sir John Dulwich	Henry Wynnebury
Name of freeholder	
John A Neve	William at Lythe
John Ashcombe	John Masoun
John Averay	Robert Mum
John de Balne	Hugh Netelfolde
William Boccrere, jnr	Thomas Noble
Robert Bonet	John Ode
Richard Busche	William Palmere
John Carpenter	Thomas at Plesshette
John Chapman, snr	Thomas Rede
John at Chert, jnr	John Saghiere
Thomas Chesman	Thomas at Sandhulle
William Coupere	Sir Robert Snokeshull, holding land formerly Edward at Sonde's
Richard Deth	Hugh at Sonde
William Drynkewater	Richard at Sonde
Richard Gylemyn	Roger Stub
Nicholas at Hambrech	John Tannere
William at Hambrech	Richard Tepeham
Ralph at Heghelonde	Robert Tepeham
Adam at Homwode	Thomas Tournour
William Inchered	Robert de Weston
Laurence Ingylby	Adam Whyting
William Kymere	John Wyntersulle
Richard at Lese	Roger Yonge
Thomas at Lompulle	

Appendix D

Names of those on the manor paying pannage in 1365-6, arranged alphabetically.

Name	Swine	Amount	Dorking	Walde
John A Neve	3	3d	✓	
John Ashcombe	/	/	✓	
Walter Bakere	2	4d [sic]	✓	
John de Balne	1	1d	✓	
Thomas Barbour	2	2d	✓	
Robert at Bere	2	2d		✓
William Bourere, snr	4	4d	✓	
William Bourere, jnr	2	2d	✓	
Robert at Bourne	1	1d	✓	
Richard Brekespere	1	1d		✓
William Brekespere	4	4d		✓
John Brokere	1	1d	✓	
Stephan Broman	2	2d		✓
William Broman	2	2d		✓
Alice Brugge	1	1d	✓	
Richard Busch	2	2d	✓	
John Carpenter	2	2d	✓	
Thomas Caas	1	1d	✓	
William Caas	1	2d [sic]	✓	
John Chapman	1	1d	✓	
Henry Charesmore	3	3d		✓
John at Chert, snr	5	5d	✓	
Walter at Clerhole	2	2		✓
Adam Clerk	6	6d		✓
Robert Clerk	7	7d		✓
Isabelle Coillard	1	1d	✓	
John Cokyr	2	2d	✓	
Avelina Colville	1	1d	✓	
Richard Deth	3	3d	✓	
Stephen Dighere	1	1d	✓	
John Donnere	1	1d	✓	
William Drynkewater	2	2d	✓	
Peter Flecchere	1	1d	✓	
Thomas Fust	1	1d	✓	
William Gauge	1	1d		✓
John Geffray	1	2d [sic]	✓	
John Godwyne	2	2d	✓	
Richard Gylemyn	1	1d	✓	

Name	Swine	Amount	Dorking	Walde
Gilbert at Hacche	1	1d		✓
Nicholas at Hambreche	4	4d	✓	
William at Hambreche	1	1d	✓	
Ralph at Heghlond	3	3d	✓	
Richard Henhurst	2	4d [sic]		✓
Nicholas Henle	3	3d	✓	
Stephan at Holoweye	2	2d	✓	
Adam at Homwode	3	3d	✓	
John Hotte	1	1d	✓	
John at Hulle	2	2d		✓
Laurence Ingylby	2	2d	✓	
John Kene	1	1d	✓	
William Kymere	2	2d	✓	
William Langshete	2	2d		✓
Thomas at Lompulle	3	3d	✓	
William at Lythe	5	5d	✓	
John Masoun	2	2d	✓	
Stephan at Mesbroke	4	4d		✓
Robert Mum	5	5d	✓	
William Mum	2	2d	✓	
Hugh Netelfolde	3	3d	✓	
Thomas Noble	1	1d	✓	
John Ode	5	5d	✓	
Henry Oslak	1	1d	✓	
William Palmere	2	2d	✓	
John at Pleystowe	5	5d		✓
R[obert] at Pleystowe	2	2d		✓
Gilbert Proteriche	5	5d	✓	
Richard Pynshagh	1	1d	✓	
Thomas Rede	1	1d	✓	
Robert at Risbrugge	3	3d		✓
William at Risbrugge	3	3d		✓
Thomas Sandhulle	4	4d	✓	
John Smyth	2	2d	✓	
Richard at Sonde	1	1d	✓	
Juliana Spicer	6	6d	✓	
Roger Stub	1	1d	✓	
John Tannere	2	2d	✓	
Richard Tepeham	1	1d	✓	
Thomas Tournour	1	1d	✓	

Name	Swine	Amount	Dorking	Walde
John Upbroke	4	4d		✓
Robert de Weston	8	8d	✓	
John Wodeward	7	7d	✓	
Adam Whytyng	1	1d	✓	
Roger Yonge	1	1d	✓	

Names of those on the manor paying to drive their beasts into the Homwode in 1365-6.

Name	Beasts	Amount
William Ansty	1 horse	2d
William Athelard	1 horse	2d
John at Balne	3 horses	6d
	2 bullocks	2d
William Bourere	6 draught animals	6d
William Broman	3 horses	6d
John at Chert	4 bullocks	4d
John at Chert, snr	30 ewes	3d
William Coupere	2 horses	4d
John Godwyne	2 mares	4d
William de Hambreche	4 bullocks	4d
Adam at Homwode	2 horses	4d
Thomas at Lompulle	3 bullocks	3d
John Ode	4 bullocks	4d
Leticia Pouke	4 cows	4d
Thomas Rede	2 horses	4d
John Saghiere	1 horse	2d
Hugh at Sonde	3 horses	6d
Juliana Spicer	5 bullocks	5d
Adam Squyer	1 horse	2d
Roger Stub	2 horses	4d
	2 bullocks	3d [sic]

Appendix E

Customary tenants fined in 1370 regarding mill soke,
arranged alphabetically.

Name	Amount
John [Balne]	12d
Robert at Bere	12d
Richard Brekespere	18d
Stephen Brouman	12d
William Brouman	18d
John Brugesulle	18d
John at Chert	18d
William at Chert	12d
Adam Clerk	2s
Thomas Fust	12d
John at Garston	2s
John Godwyne	12d
Gilbert at Hacche	18d
Margery at Hacche	18d
Stephen at Holoweye	12d
John at Hulle	18d
William at Hulle	12d
Adam at Langshete	18d
Henry Langshete	18d
William at Langshete	2s
Maurice at [Lythe]	18d
Agnes Mesbroke	18d
William Noble	12d
Adam Peter	12d
Walter Peter	18d
Robert at Pleystowe	18d
William Renger	12d
William Rogger	18d
Roger at Rugge	18d
Robert at Risbrugge	18d
William, son of Robert Risbrugge	12d
William Risbrugge	18d
Richard Sket	12d
Richard Skynnere	12d
Thomas Taylour	18d
Robert at Upbroke	18d
John Wadelshurst	12d

Appendix F

The 1381 poll tax return for Dorking, arranged alphabetically and by household (Fenwick (2001), pt 2, pp.553-555). Data in square brackets corrected by the author.

Household	Name	Role	Amount
A Neve	John at Nene	Fishmonger	---
	Matilda	His wife	
	Matilda Laurens	*Serviens*	4d
Aroun	Henry Aroun	Labourer / smallholder	12d
Ashcombe	John Ascombe	Holder of land	2s
	Rose	His wife	
Ashcombe	Roger Ayscombe	Holder of land	2s
	Agatha	His wife	
Averay	John Averay	Fletcher	2s 8d
	Joan	His wife	
Bacheler	[Roger] Batcheler	Weaver	2s
	Agnes	His wife	
Bakere	Walter Bakere	Holder of land	6d
	Margery	His wife	
Bal	John Bal'	Brewer	4s
	Matilda	His wife	
Bal	John Bal', snr	Labourer / smallholder	6d
Balcombe	Richard Balcombe	Labourer / smallholder	12d
	Alice	His wife	
Belde	Robert Belde	Holder of land	2s
	Milsant	His wife	
Belde	William Belde	Holder of land	2s
	Beatrix	His wife	
Bemond	John Bemond	Cobbler	2s 6d
	Matilda	His wife	
Bonet	John Bonet	Fletcher	12d
	Alice	His wife	
Bonet	Thomas Bonet	Holder of land	2s 6d
	Isabelle	His wife	
	John	Son of Thomas Benet	2s
	Richard	Son of Thomas Benet	
Bourere	William Bourer	Holder of land	12d
	Avelina	His wife	
At Bourne	Agnes at Burne	Spinster	12d
Bradele	Emma Bradele	Spinster	12d
Bradele	John Bradele	Holder of land	12d
Bradele	Thomas Bradele	Holder of land	2s
	Mabel	His wife	

Household	Name	Role	Amount
Brekespere	William Brekespere	Labourer / smallholder	12d
	Edith	Wife of William Brekespere	12d
Brekespere	Joan Brekespere	Labourer / smallholder	12d
Brokere	John Broukere	Holder of land	2s
	Isabelle	His wife	
Bruggesulle	John Brugeshull'	Labourer / smallholder	18d
	Margery	His wife	
Bruggesulle	William Brugeshull'	Labourer / smallholder	12d
Busche	Richard Bust'	Weaver	3s 6d
	Margery	His wife	
	Alice	*Serviens*	12d
	Margery	*Serviens*	
Caas	Dionisia Caas	Spinster	12d
Caas	Thomas Caas	Brewer	2s 6d
	Joan	His wife	
Caas	William Caas	Smith	12d
Carpenter	John Carpenter	Holder of land	2s 6d
	Katherine	His wife	
Charesmore	John Charysmour	Labourer / smallholder	2s
	Alice	His wife	
Charesmore	Thomas Charysmour	Labourer / smallholder	12d
	Alice	Wife of Thomas Charysmour	12d
Charesmore	Walter Charysmour	Holder of land	2s
	Isabelle	His wife	
At Chert	John at Churt'	Holder of land	2s
	Cristina	His wife	
Clerk	Adam Clerk	Holder of land	3s 2d
	Agnes	His wife	
	Robert	His son, *serviens*	4d
	Alice or Margery	Wife of Robert Clerk	12d
Clerk	Robert	Holder of land	12d
	Alice or Margery	Wife of Robert Clerk	12d
Cok	Alice Cok	Spinster	4d
Cotham	John Cotham	Labourer / smallholder	12d
Coupere	William Coupere	Innkeeper	2s 6d
	Margery	His wife	
Coytere	John Coytere	Labourer / smallholder	2s
	Agnes	His wife	
Cranle	William Cranle	Labourer / smallholder	18d
	Emma	His wife	

Household	Name	Role	Amount
Dauwe	John Dauwe	Cobbler	2s 6d
	Margery	His wife	
At Dene	John at Dene	Holder of land	3s
	Matilda	His wife	
	John Coker	*Servient'*	12d
	William Coker	*Servient'*	
Deyere	Stephen Deyere	Brewer	12d
Dyfforde	John Dyfforde	Fletcher	6d
Elmeshale	William Elmeshale	Brewer	12d
	Cristina	His wife	
Fisher	John Fyshere	Baker	12d
Flechynhurst	Richard Flechynhurst	Labourer / smallholder	12d
At Flushe	Isabelle at Flushe	Spinster	12d
At Flushe	Thomas at Flushe	Labourer / smallholder	12d
Fust	Katherine Fust	Spinster	12d
Gauge	William Gange	Holder of land	18d
Godefray	John Godefray	Tailor	2s
	Alice	His wife	
Godwyne	William Godwyne	Holder of land	2s 6d
	Isabelle	His wife	
Gylemyn	Richard Gybayn	Holder of land	12d
At Hambreche	Alice at Hambreth'	Spinster	6d
At Hambreche	William at Hambreth'	Labourer / smallholder	12d
Heggere	William Hegere	Labourer / smallholder	12d
At Heghlond	Ralph at Hegelond	Holder of land	2s 8d
	Amice	His wife	
	Alice	His *serviens*	4d
Henhurst	John Henhurst	Brewer	2s
	Alice	His wife	
Henhurst	Richard Henhurst	Brewer	2s 4d
	Alice	His wife	
Henhurst	Richard Henhurst	Labourer / smallholder	12d
Henle	Nicholas Henle	Holder of land	3s
	Agnes	His wife	
	Alice Stonere	*Serviens*	6d
	John Tepham	*Serviens*	6d
Henle	Robert Henle	Butcher	12d
	Petronilla	His wife	
At Holoweye	Stephen at Holewey	Holder of land	2s
	Avelina	His wife	

Household	Name	Role	Amount
At Homwode	Adam at Homwode	Holder of land	2s 8d
	Isabelle	His wife	
	William at Dene	*Serviens*	4d
Hotte	John Hutte	Labourer / smallholder	2s
	Alice	His wife	
At Hulle	John at Hull'	Holder of land	12d
	Alice	His wife	
	John	Son	12d
At Hulle	William at Hull'	Holder of land	18d
	Alice	His wife	
Inchered	William Incherd	Butcher	2s
	Dionisia	His wife	
Ingylby	Laurence Sherman	Fuller	12d
Kempe	Roger Kempe	Tailor	2s
	Alice	His wife	
Kene	Alice Kene	Brewster	18d
Kene	Beatrix Kene	Spinster	6d
Kene	Walter Kene	Baker	12d
Kentyng	John Kyntyng	Labourer / smallholder	2s
	Isabelle	His wife	
Kymere	William Kymere	Weaver	2s
	Joan	His wife	
Langshete	Maurice Langshete	Labourer / smallholder	2s
	Isabelle	His wife	
Langshete	Roger Langshete	Holder of land	20d
	Alice	His wife	
Langshete	William Langshete	Holder of land	2s 8d
	Alice	His wife	
	Giles Langshete	*Serviens*	4d
At Lompulle	John at Lompunte	Labourer / smallholder	12d
At Lompulle	Thomas at Lompute	Carpenter	18d
	Isabelle	His wife	
Lyne	John Lyne	Carpenter	12d
Lythiere	William Lythere	Carpenter	2s
	Margery	His wife	
Masoun	John Mas...	Mason	2s
	Matilda	His wife	
At Mesbroke	Walter at Mysbroke	Holder of land	2s
	Agnes	His wife	
At Monte	Henry at Monte	*Serviens*	2s 4d
	Edith	His wife	

Household	Name	Role	Amount
At Monte	William at Monte	Holder of land	2s 8d
	Lucy	His wife	
	Peter at Monte	*Serviens*	4d
Mum	William Mum	*Servient'*	16d
	Alice	His wife, *servient'*	
At Naldrot	John at Naldrot	Holder of land	2s
	Agnes	His wife	
Netelfolde	Peter Netelfold	Labourer / smallholder	12d
Noble	John Noble	Butcher	2s
	Agnes	His wife	
Noble	John Noble	Tanner	12d
Noble	Matilda Noble	Spinster	12d
Noble	Thomas Noble	Butcher	2s
	Joan	His wife	
Ode	John Ode	Draper	5s
	Dionisia	His wife	
Olyne	Gilbert Clyve	Weaver	18d
	Henry	Son	
Palmere	William Palmere	Brewer	2s 6d
	Beatrix	His wife	
Person	William Person'	Labourer / smallholder	12d
Peter	Walter Petur	Holder of land	18d
	Joan	His wife	
Peverell	John Parevell'	*Serviens*	6d
Peverell	William Peverel	Labourer / smallholder	12d
At Pleystowe	John at Plestowe	Holder of land	2s 6d
	Alice	His wife	
Pouke	Leticia Pouke	Spinster	12d
Proteriche	Alice Protherych'	Spinster	12d
Proteriche	Gilbert Proterych'	Holder of land	2s
	Juliana	His wife	
Pynshagh	Richard Pynshagh'	Tailor	12d
	Alice	His wife	
Pype	Alice Pype	Spinster	12d
Pype	Walter Pype	Miller	12d
Pypyn	Roger Pypyn	Labourer / smallholder	12d
Rede	Thomas Rede	Holder of land	2s
	Agnes	His wife	
At Risbrugge	Robert at Rysbrug	Holder of land	2s
	Joan	His wife	

Household	Name	Role	Amount
At Risbrugge	William at Rysbrug	Holder of land	2s
	Felicia	His wife	
	William	Son of William at Rysbruge	12d
Rogger	Roger Rogger'	Holder of land	2s 8d
	Agnes	His wife	
	John	*Serviens*	4d
Rogger	William Rogger	Holder of land	2s
	Edith	His wife	
At Rushett	Isabelle at Ryshete	---	12d
At Sandhulle	Thomas at Sondhull'	Holder of land	2s
	Matilda	His wife	
Shaldeforde	John Shaldeforde	Labourer / smallholder	4d
Shete	Robert at Shete	Carpenter	2s
	Alice	His wife	
Sket	Richard Skot	Holder of land	2s
	Matilda	His wife	
Skynnere	Richard Skynnere	[Butcher]	12d
Smyth	Richard Smyth	Smith	6d
	John	His *serviens*	6d
Smyth	Thomas Smyth	*Serviens*	2s
	Matilda	His wife, *serviens*	
Sneller	John Snell'	*Serviens*	12d
Snodwyne	Thomas Snodewene	Miller	12d
At Sonde	Alice at Sonde	Holder of land	18d
	Isabelle	*Servient'*	12d
	Ralph	*Servient'*	
At Sonde	Elizabeth at Sonde	Brewster	12d
At Sonde	Henry at Sonde	Holder of land	18d
At Sonde	Hugh at Sonde	Holder of land	2s 6d
	Agnes	His wife	
At Sonde	Robert at Sonde	*Servient'*	2s
	Alice	His wife, *servient'*	
Sorel	Margery Sorel	*Serviens*	4d
Spicer	Richard Spycer	Labourer / smallholder	12d
Squier	Thomas Skyer	Labourer / smallholder	12d
Stub	Robert Stub	Labourer / smallholder	12d
Sutor	John Soutere	Labourer / smallholder	6d
Sutor	Richard Sutore	Labourer / smallholder	12d
Syre	Joan	Wife of John Syre	12d

Household	Name	Role	Amount
Taillour	Isabelle Taylour	*Serviens*	2s
	William Taylour	*Serviens*	
Taillour	John Taylour	Holder of land	2s
	Edith	His wife	
Taillour	John Taylour	Labourer / smallholder	12d
	Agnes	Wife of John Taylour	12d
Tannere	John Tannare	Tanner	3s 8d
	Joan	His wife	
	Richard	Son	6d
	John Coker	*Serviens*	6d
Tannere	William Tannare	*Servient'*	2s
	Alice	His wife, *servient'*	
At Temple	Walter at Temple	Labourer / smallholder	12d
Tepeham	Richard Tepeham	Holder of land	2s 6d
	Alice	His wife	
Thurbarn	John Turbar	Holder of land	18d
	Alice	His wife	
Tournour	Thomas Tornour	Labourer / smallholder	18d
	Juliana	His wife	
Upbroke	John Upbrok	Holder of land	2s 8d
	Isabelle	His wife	
	John	His *serviens*	4d
	Edith	Daughter of John Upbrok	12d
Wadelshurst	John Watelshurst	Holder of land	12d
Walshe	John Walch'	Labourer / smallholder	2s
	Alice	His wife	
Webbe	Thomas Webb'	----	12d
Webber	Thomas Webber	Weaver	2s 6d
	Agnes	His wife	
White	William Whyte	Labourer / smallholder	12d
Whytyng	Adam Whytyng	Brewer	2s 8d
	Matilda	His wife	
	Ralph	His *serviens*	4d
Wynterfold	John Wynterfold	Labourer / smallholder	12d
Wyvenhoe	Matheus Wynenhue	Tailor	12d
Yonge	Roger Yonge	Baker	2s 8d
	Alice	His wife	
	John Haurin [Harm?]	*Serviens*	12d
Yonge	Stephen Yonge	Labourer / smallholder	12d
	Pykston'	Holder of land	12d
	Edith	His wife	

Index of Persons

Compeden (le)
    Maurice 54
    Thomas 62, 66
Conygrove (at), Thomas 54, 67
Cotham, John 88, 92
Couper(e)
    John 67f
    William 90, 108f, 144
Coter / Coytere
    John 136, 139
    Richard 116
Crese, William, vicar of Dorking 145
Crispin
    Isabelle 39
    William 44
Crul
    Gilbert 43
    Gilbert (II) 43
Cultrix, Juliana 44
Dalby, John, chaplain of Capel 145-6
Dawe (at) / Dauwe
    John 122
    John II 141
De Arderne, John, vicar of Dorking 69, 77
De Balne
    John 90f, 109, 117
    Robert, rector of Dorking 71
De Barre, Joan, countess of Surrey 72, 85, 94
De Blakelond(e), William, vicar of Dorking 69, 77
De Bletchingley, John 49
De Boklaunde, John 49
De Bradele, Thomas 10, 13
De Brecham, Roger, vicar of Dorking 118
De Clare
    Bogo 48
    Hugh 15
De Dorking
    John 50
    John (II) 76
    Maurice 75
    Odo 49

De Dorking, cont.
    Ralph 49
    Richard 67
    Richard (II) 76
        Matilda, his widow 76
    Robert 76
        Idonia, his wife 76
    Roger 68
    William 76
        Agnes, his wife 76
De Durfolde, Albreda 62
De Ewekene
    Maurice 27, 37, 39
        Isabelle, his daughter 39
        Maurice, his son 39, 60, 75, 95, 105
            Lucy, his daughter 95, 140
        William, his son 39
De Fernore, Ralph 24
De Fifehead, Philip 77
De Florence, Clerekyn 27
De Freton, Roger 105
De (la) Garstone
    Edward 28
    Gilbert 11
    William 70
De Grenestede, William 54
De Guldeford
    John 75
    Robert 65
        Matilda, his wife 65
De Habitone, Henry, vicar of Dorking 69
De Hechurst, Peter 96
De Hengham, Ralph 40
De Honeton, Richard 48
De Honilane, Ralph 76
De la Lofte, Agnes 44
De Lancaster, Thomas 72
De London, John 14
De Lustreforde, Walter 28
De Malemeyns, Nicholas 11-12, 104
De Malmesbury, John, rector of Dorking 71

Ingylby, Laurence 89, 91
Inwyn, John 142
Isemonger
    Peter 27, 44
    William 61
Janeway, William 61
Jerconville
    Roger 54, 127
    Thomas, lord of Abinger 117
Jolyfbon, John 92
Kempe
    John 13-14
    Roger 141
Kene
    Alice 125, 141, 144, 146
    Beatrix 142
    Peter 54, 67
    Richard 67, 97
        Rose, his widow 97
            John, her son 88, 92, 97, 103, 108-9
    Robert 122, 126
    Walter 122, 141
Kentyng
    John 105, 108f
        Joan, his first wife 105
        Isabelle, his second wife 105
    Stephen 67
Kymere, William 141
Kynge
    Peter 90
    Robert 66
Kyngenho, John, of Mickleham 93
Kyngesfolde (de)
    John 117, 137, 147-8
    Margery 13
Langshete (de)
    Adam 31
    Adam (II) 101
    Henry 60
    Henry (II) 101, 108
    Isabelle 154

Langshete, cont.
    Margery 133f
    Robert 31
    Roger 60
    Roger (II) 124, 145f, 146
    William 30
    William (II) 101, 128
Latymer (le), William 53
Latyn, Thomas 88
Laurence, Matilda 139
Lenkenore, Richard 98
Lese (at), Richard 95
Lompulle (at), Thomas 109, 112, 125, 142
Lote (at), Richard 66
Lovel (see also Strode)
    Hugh 40, 60
    Ingerham 40-1
        Emma, his daughter 40-1
    Peter 40, 75
        Alice, his widow 40
        Peter, his son 40-1
    Walter 40
        Agnes, his granddaughter 40
Loxle, Robert, royal escheator 147
Luwyns, John 126
Lyn(n)e
    John 142
    Laurence 55
Lyth(e) (at)
    Adam 145f, 146
    Alice 33
    Maurice 33
    Maurice (II) 102
    William 102
        Margery, his wife 102
Lythiere
    John 152
    Margery 126
    William 112, 142
Mareschal (le), Robert 76
Masoun, John 88, 130, 142

Page
    Henry 67f
    Robert 28
      Agnes, his wife 28
Pakyn, William 153
Palmere
    William, warrener 110, 127, 131-2, 144, 152
      Beatrix, his wife 132
Paon, William 62
Park (at)
    Matilda 105f, 108f
    Robert 105
Paton, William, of Leatherhead 87
Patterne, William 142
Payne, John 65
Pebelowe, John, earl's clerk 122
Peletor – see Skynnere
Person, William 139
Pe(y)ter
    Agnes 103
    Stephen 63
      Walter, his son, reeve of Dorking 63, 89, 91,
Peverell   97, 111, 126, 145f
    John 139
    William 139
Peyto(w)
    William, rector of Buckland 113
    Sir William, earl's receiver 130
Pirie, William 15
Pistur (le) - see Baker(e)
Plesshette (at), Thomas 96, 101
Pleystowe (at, de la)
    Hugh 30, 39, 60
    John 96, 101, 133
    Robert 31, 39, 67
    Robert (II) 101, 152
    Thomas 153
    Walter 153
Pouk(e)
    John 28
    Leticia 142

Pris / Priest (le), William 28, 34
Proteriche (de) / Proterych
    Alice 142
    John 20, 31-2
    John II 153
Pruut, Peter 67f
Pynchere, Richard 109
Pynkehurst, Adam 106
Pynshagh
    Richard 141
      Alice, his wife 141
Pype
    Alice 142
    William 143
Pypyn
    Roger 123, 126, 137
      Alice, his wife 137
Quarreor
    John 43
      Agnes, his widow 43
    Thomas, chaplain 105
Rede (de la,le)
    Odo 31f
    Peter 11, 39, 50, 65
    Ralph 29, 39, 140
      Emma, his daughter 29
    Simon 29
    Thomas 28
    Thomas (II) 87, 94-5, 97, 139f, 140, 155
    William 34, 37
Renger
    Adam 7, 34
      William, his son 7, 19, 23, 34
    William (II) 103
Risbrugge (at)
    John 31
    Richard 133f
    Robert 88, 101, 128, 139f, 145f
      Joan, his wife 101
      William, his son 101

Those without surnames

Catherine of Leatherhead 144
Master Elias of St Albans 70
Emma, daughter of Rose 44
Henry, chaplain of Capel 32, 47
Henry, earl's steward 51
Master James of Spain 70
John, vicar of Send 117
Sir Oliver, earl's chaplain 23
Prior of Reigate 12, 96
Prioress of Kilburn 29
Richard, rector of Dorking 48
Brother Roger 68
Master Roger 68
Brother Walter 68
William, priest of Dorking 48
William, rector of Bookham 14
William, reeve of Dorking 16

General Index

Bibliography

Primary Sources

AC = archive of the Duke of Norfolk at Arundel Castle
BL = British Library
DM = Dorking Museum archive
HRO = Hampshire record office
MA = Metropolitan archive
PRO = National Archive
SRO = Surrey record office

Manorial documents

Accounts for the Manor of Dorking

1262-3 (AC A1776)
1299-1300 (SRO 9311/1/3)
1329-30 (AC A1775)*
Michaelmas 1376 – 24th January 1376/7 (AC A1776)
1380-1 (AC A1777)
1381-2 (AC A1778)
1386-7 (AC A1779)*

Accounts for the Manor of East Betchworth 1299-1300 (SRO 9311/1/5)

Court rolls of the Manor of Dorking

1282-3 (AC M731)*
1342 & 1344-5 (AC M732)*
1365-6 (AC M733)*
1381-3 (AC M442)
1384-5 (AC M734)*
16thC extracts from court rolls 1341 to 1573 (AC M810)

*also available in transcription by Rev O'Fflahertie (SRO SYA 2/3)

Extent of the Manor of Dorking

16thC copy of 1307 text (AC M801)
notes by William Bray (SRO G85/41/1)

Extract book of the Manor of Dorking

notes by William Bray on copyhold and freehold property (SRO 196/3/1)

Survey of the Manor of Dorking

transcript of 1649 survey (DM R116/1)
copy of 1649 map by Beryl Higgins (see DM website)

Deeds relating to the Manor of Dorking

BL 8793, 8794, 9000, 9002, 9003, 9004, 9006, 9007, 9008, 9011, 9012, 9015, 9016, 9017, 9018, 9019, 9037, 9038, 9051, 9201, 18557, 18558, 18560, 18563, 18566, 18571, 18581, 18597, 18603, 18612, 18613, 18616, 18618, 18622, 18629, 18630, 18645, 18663 & 18665. (Photos at DM (R308 1-38 & 40).)

SRO K43/57/2, K43/57/27, K43/57/36, K43/58/9 & K43/58/15.

Notes by William Bray on several deeds, mostly to do with the Manor of Bradley (SRO G85/2/6).

Other documents

Debts: PRO C241/27/111, C241/81/164, C241/82/115, C241/123/120, C241/145/124 & C241/175/47.

Information on the Dutch House and its site (1996) (DM R734).

Notification of annual pension granted by Reigate Priory to St Swithun's Priory (HRO DL/A2/23).

Register of Adam de Orleton, bishop of Winchester, pts 1 & 2 (HRO 21M65/A1/6 & 7).

Sales particulars for the freehold manor of Dorking (1921) (DM S1603).

Testament of Gunnild at Dene (BL Add Ch 17295).

Wills: PRO 11/3/362, 11/5/121, 11/8/432 & MA DW/PA/7/002 f.iid.

Published sources

Accounts for the Manor of Esher in the Winchester Pipe Rolls. Surrey Record Society XLVI (2018).

Calendar of Early Mayor's Court Rolls, 1298-1307. London: HMSO (1924).

Calendar of Inquisitions Misc (Chancery)   *Richard II, vol V 1392-1399.* London: HMSO (1963).

Calendar of Inquisitions Post Mortem   *Richard II, vol XV.* London: HMSO (1970).

  Henry VI, vol XXV. London: Boydell Press (2009).

Calendar of the Close Rolls   *Edward II, vols II to IV 1313-1327.* London: HMSO (1893–98).

  Edward III, vol VIII 1346-9. London: HMSO (1905).

Calendar of the Coroners Rolls of the City of London 1300-1378. London: Richard Clark (1913).

Calendar of the Fine Rolls   *Richard II 1377-1383.* London: HMSO (1926).

Calendar of the Letter Books of the City of London A to H, 1275-1399. London: HMSO (1899-1907).

Calendar of the Liberate Rolls   *Henry III, vol I 1226-1240.* London: HMSO (1916).

Calendar of Papal Registers relating to Great Britain and Ireland, vol I 1198-1304 & vol III 1342-1362. London: HMSO (1893).

Calendar of the Patent Rolls   *Edward II, vols I to V 1307-1327.* London: HMSO (1892-1904).

  Edward III, vols I to XVI 1327-1377. London: HMSO (1891-1916).

  Richard II, vols I to II 1377-1385. London: HMSO (1895-1897).

  Edward VI, vol III 1549-1551. London: HMSO (1925).

Calendar of Wills proved and enrolled in the Court of Hustings, London, pt 1 1258-1358. London: HMSO (1889).

Domesday Book. London: Penguin Books (1992).

Liber Albus, Liber Custumarum et Liber Horn, vol II, pt II. London: Longman, Green, Longman & Roberts (1860).

Pedes Finium or fines relating to the County of Surrey. Surrey Archaeological Society extra vol I (1881).

Petitions to the Pope 1342-1419. London: HMSO (1896).

Placita de Quo Warranto temporibus Edward I, II & III. London: Record Commission (1818).

The Register of John de Stratford, Bishop of Winchester 1323-1333, vols I & II. Surrey Record Society XLII & XLIII (2010 & 2011).

The Register of William Edington 1346-1366, pts 1 & 2. Hampshire Record Society VII & VIII (1986 & 1987).

The Registers of John de Sandale and Rigaud de Asserio, Bishops of Winchester 1316-1323. Hampshire Record Society VIII (1897).

Registrum Henrici Woodlock, diocesis Wintoniensis, 1305-1316, vol II. The Canterbury and York Society XLIV (1941).

The Rolls and Register of Bishop Oliver Sutton 1280-1299. Lincoln Record Society XLIII (1948).

The 1258-9 Special Eyre of Surrey and Kent. Surrey Record Society XXXVIII (2004).

Statutes of the Realm, vol II. London: HMSO (1816).

The 1235 Surrey Eyre, pt 2. Surrey Record Society XXXII (1983).

The 1263 Surrey Eyre. Surrey Record Society XL (2006).

Surrey Taxation Returns: fifteenths and tenths, being the 1332 assessment and subsequent assessments to 1623. Surrey Record Society XI (1932).

Surrey Wills (Archdeaconry Court, Spoge Register). Surrey Record Society V (1921).

Taxatio Ecclesiastica Angliae et Walliae auctoritate P.Nicholai IV, 1291. London: Record Commission (1802).

Two Early London Subsidy Rolls. Acta Regiae Societatis Humanorum Litterarum Lundensis, XLVIII (1951).

Wykeham's Register, vol I. Hampshire Record Society VI (1896).

Several of the above were accessed via British History Online, archive.org or the Hathi Trust.

Secondary Sources

Ayto, J (2007). *Encyclopedia of Surnames.* London: A & C Black.

Bailey, M (1991). '*Per impetum maris*: natural disaster and economic decline in eastern England 1275-1350' in Campbell, B M S, *Before the Black Death: studies in the 'crisis' of the early fourteenth century.* Manchester: Manchester University Press.

Bailey, M (2002). *The English Manor c.1200 - c.1500.* Manchester: Manchester University Press.

Barron, C M (2017). 'The 'Golden Age' of Women' in Carlin, M & J T Rosenthal (eds), *Medieval London: collected papers of Caroline M Barron.* Kalamazoo: Medieval Institute Publications.

Barron, C M (2017). 'The Parish Fraternities of Medieval London' in Carlin, M & J T Rosenthal (eds), *Medieval London: collected papers of Caroline M Barron.* Kalamazoo: Medieval Institute Publications.

Bennett, H S (1956). *Life on an English Manor: a study of peasant conditions 1150-1400.* Cambridge: Cambridge University Press.

Bennett, J M (1986). 'The Village Ale-Wife: Women and Brewing in Fourteenth-Century England' in Hanawalt, B A (ed), *Women and Work in Preindustrial Europe*. Bloomington: Indiana University Press.

Blair, J (1980). The Surrey Endowments of Lewes Priory before 1200. *Surrey Archaeological Collections*, LXXII, 97-126.

Bothwell, J, PJR Goldberg & W M Ormrod (eds) (2000). *The Problem of Labour in Fourteenth-Century England.* York: York Medieval Press.

Bray, W (1816). An account of some customs in husbandry and the prices of various articles relating thereto, in the time of King Richard II. *Archaeologica: or Miscellaneous Tracts relating to Antiquity*, XVIII, 285.

Brayley, E W (1841). *A Topographical History of Surrey*, vols I & V. Dorking: Robert Best Ede.

Bright, J S (1884). *Dorking: a History of the Town.* Dorking: R J Clark.

Burns, D (1992). *The Sheriffs of Surrey.* Stroud: Phillimore.

Campbell, B M S (2000). *English Seigniorial Agriculture 1250 – 1450.* Cambridge: Cambridge University Press.

Corner, G R (1855). *On the Custom of Borough English.* Suffolk: Suffolk Institute of Archaeology.

Daniel-Tyssen, J R (1869). Inventories of the Goods and Ornaments of the Churches in the County of Surrey in the reign of king Edward VI. *Surrey Archaeological Collections*, IV, 1-189.

Day, M & V Ettlinger (2015). *Capel: the chapel by the spring.* Godalming: Ammonite Books.

DeWindt, A R & E B DeWindt (2006). *Ramsey: the lives of an English fenland town, 1200-1600.* Washington: the Catholic University of America Press

Faith, R (1987). 'The 'Great Rumour' of 1377 and Peasant Ideology' in Hilton, R H & T H Aston, *The English Rising of 1381.* Cambridge: Cambridge University Press.

Fenwick, C E (ed) (2001). *The Poll Taxes of 1377, 1379 and 1381: Part 1: Bedfordshire – Leicestershire.* London: Oxford University Press for the British Academy.

Fenwick, C E (ed) (2001). *The Poll Taxes of 1377, 1379 and 1381: Part 2: Lincolnshire – Westmoreland.* London: Oxford University Press for the British Academy.

Francia, S (2001). The Spice of Life? The Multiple Uses of Cumin in Medieval England. *The Local Historian*, 41.3, 203-215.

Franklin, P (1996). 'Politics in Manorial Court Rolls' in Razi, Z & R Smith (eds), *Medieval Society and the Manor Court.* Oxford: Clarendon Press.

Galloway, J A, D Keene & M Murphy (1996). Fuelling the City: production and distribution of firewood and fuel in London's region 1290-1400. *Economic History Review*, 49.3, 447-472.

Giuseppi, M S (1920). The Wardrobe and Household Accounts of Bogo de Clare 1284-6. *Archaeologica: or Miscellaneous Tracts relating to Antiquity*, LXX, 1-56.

Given-Wilson, C (1991). Wealth and Credit, Public and Private. The Earls of Arundel 1306-1397. *The English Historical Review*, CCCCXVIII, 1-26.

Harper-Bill, C (1996). *The Pre-Reformation Church in England 1400-1530.* London: Longman.

Hart, S (2010). *Medieval Church Window Tracery in England.* Woodbridge: The Boydell Press.

Harvey, B F (1991). 'Introduction: the 'crisis' of the early fourteenth century' in Campbell, B M S, *Before the Black Death: studies in the 'crisis' of the early fourteenth century*. Manchester: Manchester University Press.

Harvey, P D A (1996). 'The Peasant Land Market in Medieval England' in Razi, Z & R Smith, *Medieval Society and the Manor Court*. Oxford: Clarendon Press.

Hatcher, J (2009). *The Black Death: the intimate story of a village in crisis, 1345-1350*. London: Orion Books Ltd.

Heales, A (1883). Early History of the Church of Kingston-upon-Thames. *Surrey Archaeological Collections*, VIII, 13-156.

Hilton, R (1995). *Bond Men Made Free: medieval peasant movements and the English rising of 1381*. London: Routledge.

Hone, N J (1906). *The Manor and Manorial Records*. London: Methuen & Co.

Horne, S (2016). *Early Medieval Dorking, 600 – 1200 AD*. Dorking: The Cockerel Press.

Howard de Walden, T (1904). *Some Feudal Lords and their Seals*. London: Bradbury, Agnew & Co.

Hutton, R (1994). *The Rise and Fall of Merrie England*. Oxford: Oxford University Press.

Jackson, A (ed) (1991). *Dorking: a Surrey Market Town through twenty centuries*. Dorking: Dorking Local History Group.

Kingsford, C L (1915). *The Greyfriars of London: their history with the register of their convent and an appendix of documents*. Aberdeen: Aberdeen University Press.

Latham, R E (1973). *Revised Medieval Latin Wordlist*. London: Oxford University Press for the British Academy.

Lewis André, J (1899). Miscellaneous Antiquities of Dorking. *Surrey Archaeological Collections*, XIV, 1-18.

Malden, H E (ed) (1902-1912). *A History of the County of Surrey*, vols I-IV. London: Victoria County History.

Malden, H E (1930). The Parish and Curates of Capel. *Surrey Archaeological Collections*, XXXVIII, 171-176.

Manning, O & W Bray (1804-1814). *The History and Antiquities of the County of Surrey*, vols I–III.

Masschaele, J (2002). The Public Space of the Marketplace in Medieval England. *Speculum*, 77.2, 383-421.

Mate, M (1991). 'The agrarian economy of south-east England before the Black Death: depressed or buoyant?' in Campbell, B M S, *Before the Black Death: studies in the 'crisis' of the early fourteenth century*. Manchester: Manchester University Press.

McIntosh, M K (1988). Money Lending on the Periphery of London, 1300-1600. *Albion: a quarterly journal concerned with British Studies*, 20.4, 557-571.

Orme, N (2021). *Going to Church in Medieval England*. New Haven and London: Yale University Press.

Poos, C R, Z Razi & R Smith (1996). 'The Population History of Medieval English Villages: a debate on the use of Manor Court Records' in Razi, Z & R Smith, *Medieval Society and the Manor Court*. Oxford: Clarendon Press.

Powell, A & R (1997). *A Medieval Farming Glossary of Latin and English Words.* Chelmsford: Essex Record Office Publications.

Razi, Z & R Smith (1996). 'The Origins of the English Manorial Court Rolls as a Written Record: a puzzle' in Razi, Z & R Smith, *Medieval Society and the Manor Court.* Oxford: Clarendon Press.

Roud, S (2006). *The English Year.* London: Penguin Books.

Salzman, L F A (1953). The Property of the Earl of Arundel, 1397. *Sussex Archaeological Collections,* XCI, 32-52.

Schofield, J (2003). *Medieval London Houses.* New Haven and London: Yale University Press.

Schofield, J (2011). *London 1100-1600: the archaeology of a capital city.* Sheffield: Equinox Publishing Ltd.

Silverman, S (2011). *The 1363 English Sumptuary Law: a comparison with fabric prices of the late fourteenth century.* Electronic Thesis retrieved from https://etd.ohiolink.edu/.

Stuart, D (1992). *Manorial Records.* Chichester: Phillimore.

Trice Martin, C (1976). *The Record Interpreter.* Dorking: Kohler & Coombes.

Warner, K (2003). *The Amatory Adventures of John de Warenne.* Blogpost retrieved from edwardthesecond.blogspot.com/2007/04.

Warren, J (ed) (1990). *Wealden Buildings: studies in Kent, Sussex and Surrey.* Horsham: Wealden Buildings Study Group.

Wedgwood, A (1990). *A History of St Martin's, Dorking.* Dorking: Trustees of the Friends of St Martin's.

Wild, R & A Moir (2013). Key dating features for timber-framed dwellings in Surrey. *Vernacular Architecture,* 44, 46-61.